OTHER BOOKS BY KENNON L. CALLAHAN

Available from Jossey-Bass Publishing, Inc.

Building for Effective Mission

Dynamic Worship

Effective Church Finances

Effective Church Leadership

Giving and Stewardship in an Effective Church

Twelve Keys for Living

Twelve Keys to an Effective Church

Twelve Keys to an Effective Church: The Leaders' Guide

Twelve Keys: The Planning Workbook

Twelve Keys: The Study Guide

Visiting in an Age of Mission

Preaching Grace

Possibilities for Growing Your Preaching and Touching People's Lives

Kennon L. Callahan

Jossey-Bass
San Francisco

Unless otherwise stated, biblical quotations are from *The Holy Bible, Revised Standard Version* (copyright © Thomas Nelson & Sons). Also cited are the *King James Version* and *New English Bible* (K J V and NEB: Copyright © Christianity Today, Inc., 1965) and *New American Standard Bible* (NASB: Copyright © The Lockman Foundation, 1960, 1962, 1963, 1968, 1971, 1973).

Jossey-Bass books and products are available through most bookstores. To contact Jossey-Bass directly, call (888) 378-2537, fax to (800) 605-2665, or visit our website at www.josseybass.com.

Substantial discounts on bulk quantities of Jossey-Bass books are available to corporations, professional associations, and other organizations. For details and discount information, contact the special sales department at Jossey-Bass.

 Manufactured in the United States of America on Lyons Falls Turin Book. This paper is acid-free and 100 percent totally chlorine-free.

Library of Congress Cataloging-in-Publication Data

Callahan, Kennon L.
  Preaching grace : possibilities for growing your preaching and touching people's lives / Kennon L. Callahan. — 1st ed.
    p. cm.
  Includes index.
  ISBN 0-7879-4295-2 (acid-free paper)
  1. Preaching. I. Title.
  BV4211.2 .C245 1999
  251—dc21   98-51232

FIRST EDITION
HB Printing   10 9 8 7 6 5 4 3 2 1

Contents

This book is dedicated to the memory of Tom Shipp,
and to the future of Ed Peterson, and all the
other countless emerging pastors
across the planet whose preaching
will shape the twenty-first century.
Week after week, in the years to come,
their sermons of grace and compassion,
wisdom and experience,
wonder and joy,
new life and hope
will touch the lives of many people.
Their preaching will help people live whole,
healthy lives in good spirits,
with a love of fun and of life.
Many people will discover grace.
God bless their preaching.

Preface

This book will help you as you grow and build *your own distinctive gifts* for preaching. There are many excellent books on the art of preaching that provide helpful insights and suggestions. These books tend to propose a specific style of preaching; understandably, the style proposed is the style of preaching the author has come to in the course of his or her preaching experience. These books help you learn that particular approach to preaching.

This is a coaching book. It shares a foundational understanding of the art of preaching in our time. It helps you advance your particular strengths and competencies to share preaching with your congregation. I am primarily interested in helping you discover the way you can best share your preaching. I am less interested in advocating one approach to preaching.

As a coach, I want to help you discover and develop the approach to preaching that works for you. It may be, on occasion, somewhat helpful for you to "copy" other pastors' styles of preaching, but in general it is more helpful for you to grow forward the way of preaching that *matches you and your distinctive gifts, strengths, and competencies.*

I do quite a bit of preaching and public speaking. I have had the privilege of preaching in a vast array of settings, both with the congregations we have served in Ohio, Texas, and Georgia and with congregations across the country. These have ranged from small, strong congregations to large megachurches; they have been in rural and urban settings; they have represented a considerable variety of distinct denominational groupings. These diverse cultural environments have provided me with rich, full experiences that have both broadened and deepened my understanding of the art of preaching.

Moreover, in my consulting work I have had the privilege of hearing hundreds of sermons. The congregations with whom I serve as consultant are in an extensive array of settings and denominational affiliations. The pastors I hear preach range from those "fresh" out of seminary to some of the most experienced, respected preachers across the planet.

Thus, what I share with you comes both from my own preaching experience and from my reflections on the rich variety of sermons I have heard across the years. I believe this combination gives me a unique and helpful basis of experience and contributes to the perspective and the insights I have developed on the art of preaching.

Acknowledgments

I am grateful to the congregations I have served as pastor. Their contributions to my understanding of preaching have been generous and invaluable. I am thankful to the congregations and pastors with whom I have served as consultant. The interviews and group discussions with key leaders and grassroots persons on the subject of preaching have given me much material and many insights on preaching.

My gratitude goes out to countless pastors with whom I have worked over the years. Hearing their sermons has been greatly helpful to me. Sharing discussions on what it is like to preach in our time has been invaluable. Discovering with them new insights and resources that advance their preaching has helped me in my own preaching, and, very important, has contributed greatly to my understanding of how ministers advance and develop their preaching.

I am thankful for the pastors and key leaders who have been seminar participants. In these seminars on preaching we have had good fun and good times and have thought deeply about the nature and purpose of preaching. The conversations in these seminars have provided many excellent ideas and good suggestions.

I want to thank Julie McCoy Callahan. We met in high school, became good friends, began dating, fell in love, and got married, and we share a wonderful life together. Over the years she has been my best friend. Her wisdom and insights, her compassion and depth of understanding have contributed more to my life than I could ever express. She has given much help on each of the books I have written, which now circulate across the globe. Her contributions to this book have been particularly insightful and helpful. I am amazed, again and again, at the depth of her wisdom and the range of her understanding.

I want to thank D'Wayne Roberts, a wonderful friend and gifted administrative assistant, for her assistance in typing the manuscript. She has been helpful with many of my books, and I especially appreciate her concentrated help on this book.

Sarah Polster has served as senior editor. I have worked with many extraordinary people in my life, and I am continually impressed with her wisdom and clarity, her insights and perspective. She is, I am confident, among the very best editors in this country. I am most grateful for her many contributions to the depth and richness of the book.

I want to thank Joanne Clapp Fullagar for her expertise and competencies in bringing the book to production. She and her team deliver excellence, accuracy, and timeliness with a wonderfully competent professionalism. The people at Jossey-Bass, with their valued and competent support, are a delight to work with. Through them, this book is brought to fruition.

May this book be helpful to you in preaching grace and touching the lives of the people with whom you preach.

KENNON L. CALLAHAN
February 1999

1

Preaching When the Whole World Is a Mission Field

Words count. Words make a difference. Words help. Words hurt. Some words share grace and peace, compassion and community, healing and hope. Some words pass on anxiety and fear, anger and rage. Some words are like new life—like cooling waters in a hot desert. Some words bite—with shame and bitterness, grudge and resentment.

Some words lead us forward. Some are like heavy weights that drag us down. Some words help us live whole, healthy lives. Some words share the grace of God, the compassion of Christ, and the healing hope of the Holy Spirit.

Preaching counts. Preaching makes a difference.

Most preaching helps. Again and again, as I listen to sermons I am amazed at how helpful they are. Across the years, I have been privileged to hear many solid sermons. Most pastors preach sermons that share wisdom and encouragement. Indeed, most pastors preach more helpfully than they sometimes think they do. Sunday after Sunday, countless pastors share sermons that help their congregations. People discover the richness of the Gospel. Their lives are advanced. They find possibilities to grow forward whole, healthy lives.

Some preaching hurts. It is harmful. It does damage in people's lives. People are put down. They are taught low self-esteem. Codependent and dependent relationships result. Some preaching is harsh, demanding. Legalism and law pour forth. Rules and regulations abound. Grace is missing. Some preaching is weak, feeble. It is timid and tentative. It hardly matters in people's lives. Some preaching is simply boring, innocuous. It is the occasion for a quiet, pleasant nap after a busy, hectic week.

Most preaching shares help and hope. People discover the love of God. Grudges and resentments no longer have power over them. Forgiveness and reconciliation come. Anxiety and fear lessen. Anger and rage become strangers. Serenity and peace enter their lives. Compassion and community become good friends. Lives are richer and fuller.

God blesses us.

We live in one of the richest ages for mission the Christian movement has ever known. This is no longer a churched culture. Yet the customs, habits, and traditions of a churched culture linger long and die hard. Many practices that worked in that earlier time no longer hold sway. This is a new time. Just about the time some of us have thought life was half over and all we had to do was stay out of major trouble until the end, God comes and gives us a new day. This is a time of mission.

Many of us, growing up in this present time, have never known a churched culture. We have never experienced the notability and standing, the prerogatives and perks that a churched culture confers on the church. A churched culture is not in our bones. What we know—have known from the day we were born—is an age of mission.

In the churched culture, preaching was significant. But in that long-ago time, preaching enjoyed the prestige and pedestal of a churched culture. The preaching was frequently helpful, but, at the same time, it was able to get away with being less than fully helpful. It could count on the churched culture to deliver people to the church, whether the preaching was helpful or not. Church was part of the values of the culture. It was "the thing to do" to go to church.

In a churched culture, preaching benefited from a nearly pervasive consensus that church was important. Regrettably, in such a setting, some preaching had a tendency to become lazy, apathetic, and indifferent. It fell back on easy sayings and simple slogans. Some sermons were filled with collections of legalisms and laws. Shoulds, oughts, and musts were frequently present. Grace was missing.

If we were discussing preaching fifty years ago in a churched culture, our discussion would be different than it is today. Ministers could count on the prestige and pedestal of being in a churched culture, where the sermon was viewed as a "highlight" of the week.

The preachments of the sermons worked because they were shared in the comparative safety of a secure churched culture where pulpit and privilege went together. The sermons could be slightly pompous and preachy. The slogans and sayings could gloss over the ambiguities and agonies of life. The preaching could be pleasant and pleasing.

In our time, on the mission field God gives, preaching counts more tellingly, desperately, and significantly than in a churched culture. This is a beginning time. There is no consensus on church, or even on life. Preaching happens at the front lines.

Life is tenuous and swift, complex and confusing. There is much to distract us from what is really important. This is where preaching is at its helpful best. We long for, search for, whole, healthy lives. Preaching makes a difference.

Growing Your Possibilities

In the parable of the talents, each of the stewards is given talents by their Lord. They are free to invest and develop them in whatever ways match their strengths. They are encouraged to advance the talents they are given. There is nothing in the parable where they are told, "You must go and do it *this one specific way.*" The genius of the parable is that each steward is given the freedom to choose how to develop his own distinctive talents.

We each have our own unique gifts, strengths, and competencies for preaching. God gives us strengths sufficient for the mission of our time. I encourage you to develop your competencies for preaching in ways that work for you.

In this mission time, the following eight possibilities are helpful. As you advance some of these, you will grow forward your preaching:

- Presence
- Preparation
- Resources
- Content
- Motivation
- Delivery
- Structure
- Outcome

Among these possibilities, feel free to select the ones that match your distinctive gifts, strengths, and competencies. Grow the ones that have value in your community. Develop the possibilities you will have fun growing. Advance those that have promise for helping your preaching to benefit people— more richly and fully—with their lives and destinies.

Before we look at the eight possibilities for advancing your preaching, it will help for us to look at these foundations for preaching in our time:

- What people count on, look for, long for, is *helpful* preaching.
- Preaching is *a mutual event.*
- Preaching is *a sacrament.*
- There is *more than one way* to preach.

People Seek Helpful Preaching

A mission field invites *helpful* preaching. A churched culture grew "great" preachers. Now, I am well aware that the great preachers of that long-ago churched culture were also helpful. There is a sense in which they were great preachers *because* they were helpful. They employed the homiletic methods of the time and delivered a great sermon each Sunday, with superb elocution and oratory, rhythm and cadence, alliteration and poetry.

In the interviews, discussion groups, and planning sessions I have led over the years, what people talk about is helpful preaching. They say things like, "Two Sundays ago, what our pastor shared was very helpful to me where I am in life right now." "That sermon really helped me through a tough time." "When I was searching, a sermon helped me discover Christ." "I discovered my strengths as a result of a sermon last year." Hardly ever have I heard people say that they liked their pastor's preaching because it was a "great sermon." The focus is on *helpful* instead of *great.*

The word *helpful* is profoundly meaningful. As my editor, Sarah Polster, has wisely noted, "The way the word is usually used, it's not a very compelling descriptor. In fact, sometimes to say something is 'helpful' is to damn with faint praise." She goes on to observe, "I like [the way] you are elevating this humble word and recovering its true meaning."

In our time, the most important question for preaching is, Does the sermon *help* people with their lives and destinies in the light of the Gospel? As you are preparing your sermon, you can stay on track by asking yourself, In what ways will this sermon *help* people with their lives and destinies this Sunday in the light of the Gospel?

A few years back, when the focus was on church growth, the implicit and sometimes explicit question that pastors were told to ask themselves was, Does the sermon help grow the size of the church? Are we getting bigger? In that church growth time, pastors put upon themselves an unbearable burden by being worried about how each Sunday's sermon would help grow the size of the church.

In our time, a time of mission growth, I encourage you to focus on a worthwhile burden, one that God will help you with: think about how this Sunday's sermon will grow people's lives.

During the earliest days of the church growth movement, there was some sense in which the focus was on helping people with their lives in the name of Christ. But, regrettably, in recent times, some proponents of church growth seem to have become preoccupied with two things: (1) the only way you can grow a church is to have great preaching, and (2) be sure that most Sundays, you have a great sermon to help grow this church.

In fact, there are many means by which you can develop a strong, healthy congregation. There is no one way to do it. Moreover, people are more interested in sermons that help them with their lives than with sermons that grow churches.

Some pastors worry, Will this sermon increase or decrease worship attendance? In church growth preaching, the tendency is to focus on the church. But the churched culture is a long-lost myth that some people hope they can revive. They think, If only we could grow enough churches in this country, we could somehow recover that long-lost churched culture we had when we grew up.

Be at peace. The church is never at its best in a churched culture. The church is always at its best on a mission field. The church was born in a manger, not a castle. We are most at home in the front lines helping people with their lives and destinies in the name of Christ.

We enjoy the pedestal, the perks, the prerogatives, and the prestige of a churched culture. However, in our bones, we are uncertain whether this is where God has invited us to be or where we really belong. We are at our blazing best on a mission field.

In mission growth preaching, the focus is on living *in the world*. The focus is on helping people learn how to live whole, healthy lives *in the world*. The focus is not on helping people spend more time on more committees inside the church. What people come to church for, mostly, is for help with their lives.

We are no longer working to get people to "come back" to church. Those of us who grew up in a churched culture were taught that when a young couple gets married, maybe they will come back to church. Or, when the first baby is born will be a chance to get them to come back to church. Or, at least, by the time of confirmation, we will get them back to church.

We are now working with people who have never *been* part of a church, so how can we expect to get them to "come back"? The largest population in this country is the population of the unchurched. The largest denomination on the planet is the denomination of the unchurched. Welcome to an age of mission.

People join a congregation, not a denomination. Be at peace about denominations. Unchurched people don't even know what denominations are. Some members of a denomination that is concerned with theological niceties, bickering and fussing over this and that theological peculiarity, asked me once, "Dr. Callahan, do you think all these arguments we're having will hurt our efforts to reach the unchurched?" I said to them, "Unchurched people don't even know what you're talking about. And if they did, they wouldn't care. Post-lapse millenarianism is not fresh on their minds. What they are looking for is help with their lives."

As best you can, from week to week, share a helpful sermon. You will help people grow and advance their lives and destinies, richly and fully.

Preaching Is a Mutual Event

A sermon is a mutual event shared by the person preaching and the congregation. You can easily see this in an African American congregation. It is never quite clear whether the pastor or the congregation is doing the preaching. Both participate in the sermon. Helpful preaching is not the solitary act of one person. It is not a "Lone Ranger" event. Even the Lone Ranger was on a team with Tonto. Preaching is the shared event of the pastor and the congregation gathered to discover the good news of grace for this day and for the week to come.

A sermon is not a term paper. Most of us who are preaching as ministers have had some form of schooling. In universities and seminaries we were told to do our work individualistically. We were taught to craft well-worded, succinct, thoroughly analytical research papers with lots of references, resources, and footnotes. Many of us have spent hours upon hours crafting such papers.

Your sermon is not the term paper of the week. Give up any notion in that direction today. In school, we were asked to write research papers more than we were asked to develop sermons. We had more training on term papers. For this reason, we are sometimes tempted to deliver a term paper as the sermon of the morning. As I have visited churches and listened to preaching over the years, what I have heard from time to time in a service of worship is someone reading their most recent term paper. Fortunately, this has not happened often.

When we preach, we participate in the *corporate* sharing of the Gospel. We participate together in discovering the grace of God, the compassion of Christ, and the healing hope of the Holy Spirit. Just as we have come to understand the sense in which baptism and communion are corporate events, preaching is an equally corporate event. When preaching is done well, at the end of the service the congregation and the minister both know they have shared a rich experience together.

In interviews, again and again, when we talk about preaching, people mention the sense of being at one as the body of Christ, during and as a result of the sermon. We have all had times when we felt like that, because it has been like that.

The sermon is not a solitary, individualistic act of one person. We—minister and congregation—share the event of the sermon together. We come together in the sermon. The spirit of the sermon is corporate. When you look for this spirit, when you share it, it will be there. Preaching will be a mutual event.

Preaching Is a Sacrament

Your preaching is a sacred, holy gift in people's lives and destinies. Your preaching is a sign of grace, compassion, community, and hope. Your preaching is the outer and visible sign of

God's grace in people's inner lives. On a mission field, preaching is a sacrament.

It is through your preaching that people discover the compassion of God. It is through your preaching that people gather in the community of God's family. It is through your preaching that people discover "handles" of help and hope for the present and the future of their lives. On a mission field, the pastor and the congregation share together in the sacrament of preaching.

In the earliest years of the Christian movement, the sacraments were the sacraments of mission. With Jesus' death and resurrection, the sharing of sacramental acts grew among the new followers of the movement. At the close of the Gospel of Matthew, Jesus shares with the disciples a sacramental invitation: "Go."

I used to think this was a solemn command: "*Go.*" In my early years I preached many excellent sermons on Christ's command. Then, in my middle years, I thought of it as a stern challenge: "GO." I preached many sermons on the challenge of Christ. The sermons had the ring of attainment, accomplishment, and achievement about them. In recent times, I have thought more fully about the setting of the decisive moment told of in the Matthew text.

The disciples are bubbling over with joy and enthusiasm. This is one of the happiest times of their lives. They have finally figured out what the kingdom is all about. Their hearts are leaping up and down. They have discovered the good news. They don't know fully what to do with all their joy and wonder. They can hardly contain their sense of new life and hope.

When Jesus says, "Go," it is a joyful invitation. It is sacramental. Go and share the good news of the Gospel. Go and share God's grace as a drenching rain. Go and share your wonder and joy, your new life and hope. Go and share—with love and sacrament—the compassion, community, grace, and hope of God. Go and share this new life across the world.

The invitation "Make disciples" is really best understood as "Invite persons to discover the grace of God and become disciples." It is not a command: "MAKE." It is an invitation: "Help people discover what you have now discovered."

It took three years. There were the teachings, the crowds, the times away, the wonders, the stir and excitement of Palm Sunday, the fellowship of an Upper Room, and the dark, difficult experiences of Gethsemane and Golgotha, with hiding and fear, with Jesus' death, and the open tomb and the risen Lord. Finally, the disciples discovered the message that "Go" is a joyful, sacramental invitation.

Preaching this good news is one of the early sacraments of the church. It is an outward, visible sign of the grace of God. Christ encourages us to share in this act. The New Testament shares sacramental events of preaching. Peter is preaching in Jerusalem. Paul is preaching across the empire. He is preaching in the forum in Athens.

Why is he in the forum? Fortunately for the early congregations, there were not many church buildings to stay "inside of." The only place to share the preaching was in the world. In Athens, Paul is preaching in what had been the center of Greek civilization for eons. He is sharing a word of grace and compassion, community and hope with Athens.

In the preaching of the early disciples, many persons were helped to live rich, full lives in Christ. The sacramental character of the preaching helped people discover grace, compassion, community, and hope. The movement grew. Time passed.

In A.D. 312, the emperor Constantine won a decisive victory at the battle of the Milvian Bridge. With this victory the emperor began the process of recognizing Christianity as among the legitimate religions of the empire. This culminated in the remarkable Council of Nicaea in A.D. 325, where Constantine, even though yet unbaptized, as emperor presided over the creedal debates. The Christian movement went from persecution to pedestal.

With the blessing of the emperor, Christianity became one of the accepted, official religions of the Roman Empire. Church historians teach us that people flocked into the Christian churches. Many leading figures of Constantine's reign built church buildings across the empire. It became "the thing to do" to go to church. The church of the fourth century had all it could do to keep up with all the people who were flocking in.

Thus, after A.D. 325, the focus of the Christian movement's sacramental life became less missional. "Inside-the-church" sacraments became more the focus. When you look closely at the sacramental practices that began to emerge, you find that these sacramental events now focused on admittance and participation "inside the church."

The remnants of Constantine's churched culture have continued for a long time. Across the history of the Christian movement, there have been efforts to recapitulate that long-lost churched culture. You can see it in the Holy Roman Empire of a later time. You can find it in the ascendancy of the papacy prior to the time of Luther in 1517. You can see it in the more recent churched culture of this century. The notion of a churched culture has continued, from time to time, to come to the fore. Whenever there is a churched culture, the church tends to focus "inside the church."

But the Christian movement began in a manger—on a mission field. The Christian movement is most at home in an age of mission. The manger and the mission are in our bones. This is a mission field. We now live in one of the richest ages of mission the Christian movement has ever known. Welcome to the first century. Welcome to the twenty-first century. In our time, know this: your sermon, each week, is a sacramental event in people's lives.

There Is More Than One Way to Preach

There is more than one way to preach. Indeed, there are virtually as many ways to preach as there are persons who preach. The art is to discover the ways of preaching that match your gifts, strengths, and competencies. There are lots of ways to play golf. There is no one way that is the only *right* way to swing. You don't want the pro to teach you how he or she swings the club. You want the pro to help you find the way *you* best swing the club.

There are many ways to make quilts. There is no single way that is the *only* right way to do quilting. When you go to a quilting workshop, you want to learn from an experienced teacher so that you can develop the quilts that match your distinctive interests and strengths. I am deeply impressed, as I have participated in quilting workshops with Julie, with the instructors who again and again say, "Trust your creativity. Discover what works for you. Find what you have fun doing. Be open to discovering the possibilities that work for you."

Some of us learned a different lesson in homiletics courses. Remember the grading sheets that the class and the instructor used as someone preached a sermon? Those grading sheets were not neutral. They reinforced the belief that there is one right way to preach. Fortunately, those grading sheets are not used as much in our time.

A churched culture creates a certain style of preaching. Fifty years ago, when there was a churched culture, that style of preaching emerged. The social conformity of the times helped create the church conformity of the times, and the church conformity of the times led to the preaching conformity of the times. There was a certain principal style of preaching. You could choose from among several variations, but the underlying premise was a "churched focus."

Preaching is more crucial on a mission field than in a churched culture. In a church culture, lots of people had a church. It was "the thing to do" to go to church. In our time, people do not go to church because it's "the thing to do." People are there because they are searching, often desperately, to discover the grace of God in their lives.

It is the word of God shared as sacrament on this Sunday that helps people discover the grace, compassion, community, and hope in their lives. These sources of help bring people back to worship. They come yet another time looking for help with their lives. They do so in spite of other aspects of the church experience that may be less than positive. People will often put up with unsatisfactory parking or a crowded facility when they find something that touches their life and advances their future.

Words count. Words make a difference. Now you get your chance. Frequently this is the one chance you have—and not just for first-time worshipers. People are in a search, people are in a pilgrimage in this life, and on this specific Sunday, the word that is shared advances their lives. What you share helps people discover who they can be.

Discover your strengths. Discover a way of preaching that matches your strengths. It is important to start claiming your strengths now so that you can discover the way of preaching that matches the strengths God gives to *you,* not to someone else.

Many ministers do a better job of preaching than they think they do. They help more people with their lives than they are aware of. In the conversations, interviews, and planning discussions I have held over the years, people are deeply appreciative of the help they receive from the sermons shared in their congregations.

Most ministers want to help. Sometimes, the desire to help turns into a desire to please. Helping people and pleasing people are two distinct ventures in life. It is important to keep them distinct. It is decisive, in life, to distinguish between one's needs and one's wants. In preaching, it is important to maintain some distinction between helping and pleasing.

When we are pleasing people, it does not mean that we are therefore helping them. However, when we are displeasing people we are not necessarily helping them either. We may just be doing less than competent preaching. Their displeasure simply reflects their awareness that we are doing less than we can do.

Nonetheless, displeasing people does not always mean that we are being incompetent. Sometimes when we speak helpful words with compassion and hope, some people are not pleased. This may be a sign that we are on the right track. In working with persons who wrestle with alcoholism, I know we are frequently at the breakthrough point when the alcoholic is shouting at his loudest. In some congregations, when a particular person or a given group is not pleased with our preaching, it may be a sign that we are inviting them, constructively and positively, to give up a pattern of codependency-dependency with which they have been comfortable for years.

A minister's desire to please can also lead to the minister's becoming oversensitive to criticism. The minister hears the one complaint about a sermon as though it were a hundred complaints. The fifty positive, appreciative comments are not heard, or are heard only in a minor way. The positive reinforcement of the constructive comments is lost. The focus lingers too long on the one complaint heard as though it were a hundred.

This is one reason some ministers do not grow forward their preaching, or, when they do, they do so in a slow, cautious way. They have listened too much to the negative comments on their preaching, or, what is worse, they have listened to the silence on their preaching. Either way, they have allowed themselves to become cautious about their own growth and development in preaching.

The irony is that, week after week, ministers invite people to leave off their old ways and head to new ways, and sometimes they themselves continue in the old ways they have been preaching. If people can head to new possibilities in something as complex as life, ministers are capable of heading to new possibilities in preaching. My experience is that, given half a chance, and with wisdom and encouragement, many ministers grow forward, among the eight possibilities, the ones that match their gifts and strengths. Now, in the chapters that follow, we will look at each of these eight possibilities, so you can discover ways to advance your preaching and touch people's lives with the grace of God.

2

Presence

Your sense of presence shapes how you preach and how your sermon is received. Presence is a sense of assurance and deep-felt confidence. It is a spirit of peace and quiet power. Presence is a matter of warmth and manner, of passion and poise, of direction and bearing. It is a spirit of confidence that enables you to develop a close relationship between you and your congregation during the sermon. Presence communicates the sense that the grace of God is being genuinely shared in this sermon.

I was helping in a church. During the worship service, I had watched the pastor as he slowly, carefully, precisely, meticulously read a twenty-minute-long manuscript sermon without ever looking up once during those twenty long, long minutes. Following the service, the pastor asked me what I thought of the sermon.

I have been helping pastors and congregations a long time. I am wise enough to know that I do not talk with pastors about their sermons on Sunday. I do not even discuss them on Monday. Some pastors are simply tired. With others, there may still be some despair, depression, and anger left over from Sunday; they wish they had done better.

I dearly love A&W root beer. This particular community still has one of the old A&W root beer stands with booths and tables in an inside area. I suggested to the pastor that we visit over an A&W root beer during our Tuesday morning break to discuss the sermon. My invitation. My treat.

Tuesday morning came. We went to the A&W root beer stand. We got the large frosted mugs, ice cold. We found a corner booth and sat down. The pastor, with eager anticipation, again asked what I thought of Sunday's sermon.

Picking up a sheet of paper, holding it in front of me as though I were reading from it, I said in an easygoing way, "Where did you learn to read slowly, carefully, precisely, meticulously a twenty-minute-long manuscript sermon without ever looking up once during those twenty long, long minutes?" I said to him, "You didn't learn that in seminary. Even in seminary, they teach you to look up three times—once for each of the three points. That's what I call the Trinitarian look-up."

We thought and thought, puzzled and considered. The clue finally came when he described how during the spring semester of his senior year in seminary, he and his fiancée were married. Graduating from seminary, they went eagerly and with excitement to serve their first congregation.

The church was near enough to her parents that each Sunday for the three years they served that congregation, her parents came, smiling and beaming, to worship in their daughter and son-in-law's church. His in-laws lived just near enough that each Sunday for those three years he and his new bride went back to her parents' home after church for a Sunday meal.

As they would sit down to a lovely meal, the pastor's father-in-law, well-meaning, good-intentioned, would pull out of his inside coat pocket a little black notebook of corrections he had made while listening to his new son-in-law's sermon that morning. The grammatical errors that had been made. The sentence structure, the syntax, the synonyms, and the learned words that would improve the sermon. For those three long, long, long years, each Sunday after worship this well-meaning correcting session had taken place.

The pastor was competent and compassionate. Nevertheless, those sessions had created a pastor who, all these years later, would read slowly, carefully, precisely, meticulously a twenty-minute-long manuscript sermon without ever looking up once during those twenty long, long minutes, so that he would be sure never to make a mistake.

I took a paper napkin and drew a diagram of the worship space of his church. I then said to the pastor, "Show me where your father-in-law is sitting each Sunday." He said, "Oh, no. My father-in-law died ten years ago."

Picking up the same sheet of paper I had used earlier, holding it in front of me as though I were reading from it and without looking up, I said, "Well, he may have died ten years ago, but he is still showing up every Sunday."

And the pastor knew! He knew right where his father-in-law had sat every Sunday during those three long, long years making careful, meticulous notes in his little black notebook.

So I encouraged him, "Think of a mentor who has meant much to you during your life's pilgrimage. An encourager, a nurturer, a coach. Someone who has helped you live your life at your best. Not someone who has been correcting. Someone who has shared coaching with you, someone who has helped you to grow forward."

He thought of Dorothy, from a previous church. She was someone who had been a mentor and an encourager. I said to him, "This coming Sunday, as you look out before the sermon begins, where will Dorothy be sitting?" He said, "Oh, no. Dorothy lives clear across the state."

Picking up the same sheet of paper, holding it in front of me as though I were reading from it, without looking up I said, "Yes, and your father-in-law lives clear across the river on the other side, and he is still showing up each Sunday. If he can make it from that far away, Dorothy can be present on Sunday, too."

He knew immediately where she would be sitting. Right there, toward the center, where in the previous church, her presence, encouragement, and mentoring had meant much to him.

I said to him, "Who is a second mentor who comes to your mind? Show me where he or she will be sitting this Sunday." Jim. He knew right where Jim would be sitting—toward the front on the left side. I said, "Who is a third mentor who has helped you grow, whose encouragement and presence has meant much to you?" Sue. Without my asking, he knew exactly where she would be sitting this coming Sunday. She always slipped in just as the service began, sat on the aisle on the very back row, and slipped out just as the service ended.

I then said to him, "This coming Sunday and every Sunday hereafter, before the service begins, I want you to look out and see Dorothy and Jim and Sue. If you'll give me half a chance, I'll be sitting there too, right beside Dorothy."

A sense of peace came into his being. His face relaxed. He seemed more himself.

Then I asked him, "What was something your father-in-law enjoyed doing in this life?" "Traveling," he answered. "Well," I said, "this coming Sunday let him travel. He has probably never been to the Himalayas. He will send a postcard back saying, 'Having a great time. The mountains are really high. Remember your synonyms.'"

"The next Sunday you could let him travel to Manchuria. Not many people ever get to Manchuria. The next Sunday, you could let him travel to Mongolia. I hear it's pretty this time of year in Mongolia."

The pastor and I had a grand visit. We enjoyed a second tall, ice-cold mug of A&W root beer. We laughed and carried on.

Some time passed, and I received a letter from this pastor. He thanked me for the long-range plan we had developed together with his congregation. He thanked me for the A&W root beer. He most particularly wanted to thank me for the paper napkin. He had asked me to let him keep it. He told me in his letter that the napkin sits on his pulpit, and each Sunday before the service he looks out and sees his mentors. They are with him, and he has a sense of their presence. He has the confidence of his own presence.

God comes to us directly. God comes to us in Jesus Christ. God comes to us in the Spirit. Moreover, God comes to us in our mentors. Indeed, God sends us our mentors to help us grow forward in this life. In Hebrews 12:1, we discover these words: "Therefore, seeing we also are surrounded about with so great a cloud of witnesses, let us lay aside every weight and the sin that does so easily beset us, and let us run with perseverance the race that is set before us."

The author has in mind a stadium of witnesses. The witnesses are our mentors, encouragers, and coaches. They cheer us on, wish for us the best, and help us live life at our best.

When we sense the presence of our mentors with us, our lives have a sense of presence. We are more at peace. We draw on their wisdom. We sense their encouragement. We have a spirit of confidence and assurance. We know we are not alone. We know there are persons who love us, care for us, and encourage us. Who want for us the best in this life—and in the next.

God wants you to have a sense of presence in your preaching. Presence is not simply a matter of genetics. It is not that some people are born with it and others are not. God wants to help you, to encourage you, to help you develop a rich, full presence.

Our confidence is not in ourselves. Our confidence is in the grace of God. To paraphrase Paul, by grace we have a sense of presence, and this finally is not our own doing: it is the gift of God. This is my way of confirming that presence is not something you need to come up with all by yourself. You are not left to yourself in this endeavor. God is with you. Indeed, people with presence have a deep, abiding sense that all they are and all they have is a gift of God.

When we are caught up in the grace of God, we share our preaching with presence. What is compelling is the message we share. When we get caught up in ourselves, we become preoccupied with "how we are doing." We lose our focus on the grace of God, and we lose a sense of presence.

Presence is, in itself, preaching. One's sense of presence communicates the grace of the Gospel. One's lack of presence distracts from the grace of the Gospel. Who you are is as helpful as what you say. Someone once said, "Who you are thunders so loudly I cannot hear what you say." There is truth to that point. I say it this way: "Who you are thunders so loudly, I *can* hear what you say."

A sense of presence—of confidence and assurance—communicates the grace of the Gospel as much as the words you say, the points you make, the insights you share, and the longings you stir.

Preaching is presence. The other possibilities for growing forward your preaching—preparation, resources, content, motivation, delivery, structure, and outcome—are important. These contribute to each other. As you develop your strengths in one or two of these, the others will be helped along as well. Growth breeds growth. Strength breeds strength. At the same time, people teach me, again and again, that what they remember of a sermon is the presence of the person preaching. They may have some indirect or direct sense of preparation, resources, content, motivation, delivery, structure, and outcome. These contribute to the impact of the sermon.

They teach me that although they may not remember precisely all the points of the sermon, they do remember the person and the person's presence. They have some vague notion of what the sermon was about. What they remember is the confidence and assurance of the person who preached the sermon.

Presence is confidence and assurance, anxiety and mistakes. People with presence are frequently nervous, unsure, and uncertain. It is not that they are calm and collected, with no worries. Somehow their sense of presence helps them live through the mistakes, the anxiety, the insecurity, the worry, and the nervousness.

Anxiety advances the message. Some anxiety helps. Our anxiety, in balance, teaches us how important what we are doing is in the lives and destinies of people. Too much anxiety causes the minister and, finally, the congregation to shift the focus from the message to the anxiety. Preoccupied with anxiety, we lose the message.

People with a deep sense of presence do have anxiety. They are usually nervous as they prepare the sermon. They know how consequential this message can be in people's lives. Their anxiety rises as the time of the sermon draws near in the service. They have anxiety as they preach the sermon.

A person without anxiety either is dead or does not understand how helpful and decisive the sermon is in the lives of the persons gathered to hear it. The message is primary. The anxiety is secondary. Ministers with presence are simply not overcome by anxiety. They do not allow their anxiety to become dominant. They know that if that were to happen, the focus would be on their anxiety rather than on their message.

People who have presence frequently make mistakes. Sometimes they stumble over words and sentences. They try to say some carefully phrased sentence and botch it miserably.

They lose their sense of direction in the sermon. They forget what they were planning to say. Their mind draws a blank. They lose their train of thought and, as a result, skip whole sections of helpful material that were essential to the main message in the sermon. With a sense of presence, with a sense of the inviting, compelling grace of God, they move forward. They do not become unduly disturbed or distracted. They continue to share good news.

Ministers with a deep sense of presence do make excellent mistakes. I use the term *excellent mistakes* to affirm two things: (1) they are major mistakes, not simply minor ones; and (2) the ministers learn from their mistakes.

The mistakes may be in insight, style, grammar, or delivery. The most serious of these are mistakes in insight. We do sometimes allow ourselves to flounder in laws and legalisms. Old ways die hard. We slip back to telling and scolding rather than inviting and encouraging. We deal with excellent mistakes well when we do not take ourselves too seriously. By the same token, excellent mistakes *help* us not to take ourselves too seriously.

Presence is a spirit you can learn and develop. You can grow in yourself this sense of confidence and assurance. You can grow forward a sense of presence as you

- Remember your mentors
- Share a spirit of humor
- Do bridging with your congregation
- Focus on living in the grace of God

Mentors

Helpful preaching comes with presence. God invites us to live a life of presence surrounded by the sense of our mentors. Remember your best, most helpful mentors. Have the sense that they are with you as you live each day. Your sense of presence will grow. You are welcome to have the sense of the presence of your mentors each time you preach. They will be with you.

Further, you can build a current mentoring, coaching team of persons who will help you grow yourself. A mentor is an encourager, a coach, a nurturer, and a cheerleader. This team of three or four persons can actively mentor you now. This is not primarily a support group, a listening group, or a sharing group. They may do some or all of these things, but their primary purpose is coaching, mentoring, and encouraging.

They deliver coaching, not correcting. An example of correcting is "Stop doing this; don't do that." Coaching is more like "That's good . . . keep doing this . . . you can consider this possibility. . . ." Mentors help us find our way forward.

Look for persons like the mentors who have meant much to you in your past. Look for persons whose gifts match those you are seeking to develop. Decide which of the eight possibilities to advance your preaching you plan to develop. Share with your mentors the ones you have selected. They will share with you their wisdom, experience, and encouragement. Surrounded by the mentors from your past and a coaching team of mentors in your present, you will have a sense of presence. Your preaching will come.

Let your mentors be an informal group that you call on individually or collectively, at whatever pace works well for you, to help you grow yourself. Your team can gather as often as will help you, but not so often that it begins to deliver more help than is helpful. The art of your coaching team is to deliver just enough help to be helpful, but not so much help that its help is harmful.

You are looking for mentors who bring wisdom, who know your strengths, who make helpful suggestions, and who share encouragement. Your mentors may gather from time to time as a group. Mostly, they informally coach you on the possibilities, among the eight, that you have selected to grow your preaching.

Think about mentors in other communities as well as the one in which you now live. Think of persons whom you may not know well now but who are gifted and well known for their mentoring, coaching competencies. Modern technology—phone, mail, e-mail, fax, or an express delivery service—overcomes distance as you correspond with them. Choose what works best for you.

Sometimes the worship space in which we are preaching is half-empty. You can fill any half-empty space with your mentors as you visualize their presence, and you will fill that space with helpful preaching—the kind of preaching that helps people grow whole, healthy lives, building on the gifts, strengths, competencies with which God has blessed them. When you fill that worship space with your mentors, God will fill that space with whatever persons God sends for you to help with their lives. We have a sense of presence as we sense the presence of our mentors with us in our lives and in our preaching.

Humor

A second way ministers grow a sense of presence is to develop a rich, full sense of humor. Humor is freeing. Humor heals. Humor gives us room. Humor helps us see the relativity of many of our carefully constructed customs and habits. Humor sets us free from the staid, closed, fixed conventions with which we scrupulously surround ourselves. Humor helps us know the irony of much we hold too dear.

There is an important role for humor in preaching the Gospel. Now, humor is different from barbed ridicule. Derision and mockery have no place. Humor is not mean and satirical. It is not coarse and cynical, boisterous and raucous. Humor is good-natured and friendly. It is fun and uplifting. Humor has a good time.

I watched one pastor, partway through his sermon, stumble over his words. They came out in an inverted, confusing way. The awkwardness of the moment was that he was in the midst of a serious point. He did not become flustered or frustrated. He did not become distracted with his stumbling and confusion. He chuckled, almost to himself. He smiled at the humor in what had happened. With a good-natured spirit, he continued with the sermon.

Humor is deeper than a joke. Some ministers make it a practice, each Sunday, to begin their sermon with the most recent joke they have discovered. For many pastors, beginning with a joke or some form of humor helps them begin in a relaxed, confident manner. The downside is that this is a very predictable way of beginning.

Sharing the most recent joke, when it is good fun, is fine. It adds a good spirit. Sometimes, though, it is best shared in the sermon, rather than always at the beginning. The art of the sermon beginning is to have some newness to it each Sunday. The art is to vary the forms of humor and to place them naturally in the sermon, rather than routinely to put them at the same place.

Humor helps us not to take ourselves too seriously. A pastor who takes himself too seriously causes people in the congregation to become tense and tight, nervous and anxious. People participate in and receive the sermon more fully when they are relaxed.

Humor conveys a warmth of spirit, a sense of peace and quiet power. Humor helps us to give up being taut and rigid, worried and frazzled. We are able to see the genuine good humor in our lives. We appreciate the good fun and good times with which God blesses us.

I encourage ministers, as they preach, to relax, have fun, enjoy life, and live in Christ. The ballplayer who is determined to hit a home run on every pitch usually strikes out. Some ministers try too hard to get their point across, and, in doing so, they lose the strength of their point. People become uncomfortable over how tense and tight, nervous and anxious these ministers are.

God loves a cheerful preacher. Do not preach out of duty or obligation. The sermons will only have about them a sense of duty and obligation. Preach with a sense of joy and wonder, new life and hope, humor, good fun and good times.

Bridging

A third way to grow a sense of presence is with a principle I call bridging. The art is to discover some bridge—constructive and helpful—between you and the congregation.

In the summer of 1998, I was visiting with John Mavor, president of the Uniting Church of Australia. This was my sixth trip to Australia, and it had been arranged that John and I could have fun over lunch during one of the seminars I was leading.

John is a remarkably gifted person and a good friend. Over lunch, I asked, "John, as president of the Uniting Church of Australia, share with me one of your goals for the coming year." John said, "I hope to help congregations be more generous with first-time worshipers. To be more welcoming and accommodating. Open, helpful, receptive."

Then I asked John about his family and recent developments. He described to me his grandchild, firstborn on both sides of the clan, a grandson, born in England. A few weeks hence, he planned to be in England to baptize his new grandchild.

We talked about John's goal for the Uniting Church for about ten minutes, a brief time. We talked at some length, perhaps twenty or twenty-five minutes, of John's family and new grandson. That afternoon, as I was leading the seminar, I put the two parts of our conversation together.

I said to the participants, "Be as generous with first-time worshipers as you are with your grandchildren. Be as generous with new persons as your best grandparent is with you. Be as generous in welcoming them as your best mentors are generous with you."

I went on to describe the three grandchildren with whom God has blessed us: Blake, Mason, and Brice. When they are coming to visit with us, Julie and I think through, "Now what does Blake like for breakfast? What does Mason enjoy doing for fun? What are some of Brice's favorite activities?" Julie and I are generously flexible and accommodating. Yes, we have some boundaries, and these boundaries are warmly generous and inviting. We are welcoming, open, and generously helpful.

I shared with the seminar the generosity and openness with which my own grandparents welcomed me each time I visited in their home. I described the warmth and encouragement some of my mentors have given me across the years. I suggested that the participants relate with newcomers in the same spirit with which they relate to their grandchildren, or as their best grandparent relates to them, or as some of their mentors encourage them.

What I was doing was bridging people from their experiences with their grandchildren, their grandparents, and their mentors to the generous possibilities for relating to new persons in their congregations.

Sometimes the bridge is a common interest such as quilting, sports, art, or music. The bridge may be a common experience we have shared together, such as a mission project, a fellowship event, or a life stage through which we have passed. Sometimes the bridge may be a human hurt and hope, such as addiction or loss of a loved one, or a community interest, such as education or safety. Frequently, the bridge is something we have fun sharing together.

As we bridge from constructive, generous, positive relationships in our lives, our preaching has about it a sense of presence. Further, whenever you can bridge the material you are sharing in your sermon to the interests, needs, and life stages of your congregation, your preaching will have a sense of presence.

Living

A fourth way people grow forward a sense of presence is in their living. People who live life richly and fully, focus on their strengths rather than their weaknesses. They claim their strengths. They build on their strengths. They do better what they do best. They expand one current strength. They add one new strength. They advance their lives.

They do not allow themselves to be distracted by this or that inconsequential matter. They are not overcome by a compulsion toward perfectionism. They do not become preoccupied with their problems, needs, concerns, weaknesses, and shortcomings.

In a recent book, *Twelve Keys for Living,* I discuss this topic in depth. The central understanding of the book is this: the person who claims her strengths claims God's gifts. The person who denies her strengths denies God, denies God's gifts. Some people live half their lives looking down on themselves, thinking more poorly of themselves than they have a right to, suffering from low self-esteem. They deny God. When they now claim their strengths they claim God's gifts.

They focus on the some of the twelve keys that help them grow whole and healthy lives. They concentrate on the few "20 percenters" that deliver 80 percent of their results. I understand the principle this way: 20 percent of the things a person does delivers 80 percent of her growth, health, and wholeness; 80 percent of the things a person does delivers 20 percent of her growth and development.

People who are developing whole, healthy lives have a sense of presence about them. They live with the confidence and assurance that they are moving in a healthy direction. They have a sense of solid self-esteem. They live life with character, integrity, and honesty. Their sense of mission, compassion, community, and hope is deep and full.

They have the certainty they are headed in a constructive direction. They know they do not have all the answers. They know they have much to learn. They share their wisdom and experience with a spirit of humility and generosity.

Their preaching shares this same spirit. As a consequence, people experience them as having a solid sense of presence. It is hard for someone who is not growing forward his own life to preach with any sense of presence. Innately, he knows he has allowed himself to come to a standstill in his own growing and developing. Whether the root is despair and depression, being scared and scarred, a compulsion toward perfectionism, low self-esteem, anxiety, or fear is somewhat beside the point.

The point is simply this: people who are growing their own lives have a sense of presence as they preach. People who are not actively growing their own lives lack presence in their preaching. Their preaching tends to swing between being weak and feeble on the one hand, harsh and demanding on the other. Neither extreme is helpful.

Live the way you want to preach. Live a life of grace, and you will preach grace. Live a life of wisdom, hope, and mission, and you will preach these, with the ring of truth and experience. Presence will be with you.

Preach the way you want to live. Preach grace, and you will become grace. Preach law, and you will become law. If you preach grace, you will, more fully, live grace. What you share shapes who you become. Who you are becoming shapes what you say. The two go hand in hand. It is as we live whole, healthy lives that we develop a sense of presence, confidence, and assurance about this life and the next.

Presence is important and powerful in sharing the good news of grace in your preaching. Presence is the sense of confidence and assurance that, in this sermon on this day, the sermon is sharing the generous, holy, compelling grace of God. When we preach in this way, our preaching has a sense of peace and quiet power. Our sermon is telling and decisive. We touch people's lives. Their lives take on a sense of presence. They live life with confidence and assurance, poise and bearing, warmth and generosity, integrity and character, hope and grace.

3

Preparation

Preaching is preparation. How you prepare is how you preach. How you begin is how you end. There is a direct correlation between preparation and preaching.

A number of years ago, I was leading a seminar on preaching. A remarkable group of ministers had gathered for the event. An air of expectancy and enthusiasm filled the room. We were looking forward to good fun and good times together. As people were gathering, I had the fun of visiting with each participant. For more than a year, we had anticipated being together. The time had finally come. There was considerable excitement for our time together.

At the outset of the seminar, I listed the eight possibilities for growing one's preaching. Then I invited each person to choose his or her team partner and spend several minutes sharing with their team partner which of the eight would be most helpful to them. I was looking for some sense of which of the possibilities held their strongest interest. My thought was that, although we would discuss all eight, we would invest slightly more time in the possibilities of primary interest.

Then I asked the teams to share their interests with the whole seminar. I discovered that many of the participants were interested in resources and content. Many spoke of their hope that we would spend time on motivation and delivery. Many wanted particular help with structure and outcome. All of the participants were interested in the possibility of presence. Interestingly, all of the participants wanted us to invest considerable time on the possibility of preparation.

The seminar ran from Tuesday morning through Friday noon. I saved the discussion on preparation for Thursday morning. Given the compelling interest of the group, I wanted some time to think through, more fully, the dynamics of preparation. I also wanted the time to visit with participants in the seminar to come to a richer understanding of why their interests in the area of preparation were so strong.

In our individual conversations, some of the participants shared with me that their practice is to prepare their sermon Monday through Friday mornings in their study. Many of the participants shared with me that they begin working on their sermon on Friday or, sometimes, on Saturday, or even Saturday night. Some shared that they prepare their sermon beginning at 5 A.M. Sunday morning. These participants also shared their frustration that they could not prepare their sermons the way they had been taught to do in seminary—namely, to work on them Monday through Friday mornings.

I thought about these conversations.

On Thursday morning, I began the seminar session on preparation by saying, "Some of us have learned how to be solid marathon runners. Some of us have learned how to be excellent sprinters. These are learned patterns of behavior. This is not a genetic imprint. You and I can learn either or both behavior patterns. For whatever reasons, some of us have learned, for this time in our lives, one pattern of behavior, and some of us have learned the other pattern of behavior."

I went on to affirm that about half the people I meet in life have learned a behavior pattern of being solid marathon runners—they live their lives in a routine, regular, steady, week-by-week pattern. About half the people I meet in life have learned an excellent sprinter behavior pattern—they live their lives in short-term, highly intensive ways near the time at hand. Yes, on occasion I meet a few middle-distance runners, but, mostly, I find marathoners and sprinters.

Both the marathon and the sprinter patterns work. God blesses both. Projects can be carried out in a solid marathon behavior pattern, and projects can be carried out in an excellent sprinter behavior pattern. Solid marathon runners pack for vacation a week ahead, and they check their work several times. Excellent sprinters pack for vacation as the car is leaving the drive. Both have fun on the vacation.

Marathon runners study two hours every night. Excellent sprinters—in a short-term, highly intensive manner—study the two nights before the exam. Both make solid grades. Marathon runners tend, almost disdainfully, to regard excellent sprinters as "cramming" for an exam. From the viewpoint of excellent sprinters, they are doing what they do best.

I observed, parenthetically, that I may have saved the seminar participants who have children long hours of conversation with their kids. Parents who have learned how to be solid marathon runners frequently insist that their excellent sprinter kids study two hours every night. Their children can put in the time, turn the pages of the book, and, two hours later, remember little of what they have read. "Two hours every night" is not how sprinters do life.

In the New Testament, John is a solid marathon runner. Peter is an excellent sprinter. Both John and Peter discover Christ. John was the "beloved of Christ" and Peter was the "rock on which Christ would build his movement." Remember when the disciples discover that the stranger on the shore is Jesus? What does Peter do? He leaps out of the boat and sprints to shore! God blesses both marathoners and sprinters.

I went on to say to the seminar participants, "The reason some ministers do their sermon preparation on Friday, Saturday, and Sunday is because they are excellent sprinters. They do not find themselves drawn to a routine, regular, daily marathon style. They do short-term, highly intensive sermon preparation because that is how they do life."

The response of the persons in the seminar was extraordinary. There was the deep-felt laughter of recognition. There was warm applause. Many shared their profound appreciation. For them, the guilt had been lifted. Their guilt, over the years, of not doing sermon preparation the way they had been taught in seminary was no more. They were relieved. They were freed to do sermon preparation in the way that matches the way they do life.

Preparation is one of the possibilities with which ministers advance their preaching. You can grow your competency of preparation as you

- Develop a method of preparation that matches you
- Create a sense of balance
- Discover the place that helps you
- Advance your shepherding with your congregation

Select whichever of these you will have fun developing, and your sermon preparation will grow forward.

Methods of Preparation

As I have already suggested, two primary methods of preparation are available to you: the excellent sprinter method and the solid marathon runner method. Both methods work. The art of sermon preparation is to use the method that matches both how you live life and how your congregation lives life.

My recent research and reflections have led me to an important conclusion. I have always known that many people learn how to be solid marathon runners and many learn how to be excellent sprinters. What is new in my thinking is that, in our time, a distinctive change has taken place in the culture.

In the past, the culture reinforced the values and behavior pattern of being a marathon runner. To be sure, there were sprinters in the past, but the premium was on being a marathon runner. In the parable of the hare and the tortoise, a marathon culture wrote an ending wherein the tortoise won. The message of the culture was, Marathon runners win.

For the first time in the history of human civilization, an important shift has occurred. The nomad culture of earlier times was a marathon culture. The agrarian culture was a marathon culture. The industrial culture was a marathon culture. Our current culture is both a technological culture and an excellent sprinter culture. The culture now reinforces the behavior pattern of being an excellent sprinter.

Lots of us who learned how to be solid marathon runners are now retraining ourselves. We are learning how to become excellent sprinters. Our children and our grandchildren are teaching us how to be excellent sprinters. In this time, the primary way they are going to survive and thrive is to be excellent sprinters.

There will still be solid marathon runners. Some of our children and grandchildren will be solid marathon runners. Back in the days of a solid marathon culture, there were sprinters, and the sprinters sometimes felt like misfits. We are now in the days of a sprinter culture, and those of us who are solid marathon runners sometimes feel like misfits. That is fine, because we can learn how to be excellent sprinters.

We now live in a culture that reinforces a sprinter pattern of behavior. Many excellent sprinters discover Christ. They do so in short-term, highly intensive ways, near the time at hand. On a given Sunday, your sermon touches their hearts. They are led, that Sunday, to discover the grace of God.

Preparation shapes preaching. When someone uses a solid marathon form of sermon preparation, what will show up on Sunday is a solid marathon sermon. The sermon, steadily, routinely, will share the grace of God. When someone uses an excellent sprinter form of preparation, Sunday's sermon will be an excellent sprinter sermon. The sermon, in a short-term, intensive fashion, will share the grace of God.

Develop the method of preparation that matches both how you live life and how the people in your congregation and your community live everyday, ordinary life. Ministers who do solid sermon preparation prepare their sermons the same way they live everyday, ordinary life. When you match your preparation to the way you and your people live, you are likely to achieve your most helpful preaching.

Many—if not most—people live life in our time in an excellent sprinter pattern. Look at your congregation as it gathers for worship. You will discover long-time members who have learned how to be solid marathon runners—whose grandchildren and great-grandchildren are teaching them how to be sprinters. You will discover that an increasing number of the people you hope to reach with the grace of God are excellent sprinters.

Sprinter Preparation

I encourage excellent sprinters to do what I call four-for-three preparation. Select four days for the coming three months. For example, you might select four days in January. Go somewhere you will have fun. You do not have to go far. Some ministers do this at home. Some find a Sunday school classroom not used during the four days. Some select a local library, a meeting place, or a retreat center. Simply let it be a place you enjoy.

Use these four days to look at the coming three months, for example, February, March, and April. Do four things: study, pray, think, and relax. Do short-term, highly intensive, near-the-time-at-hand sermon preparation.

In these four days, accomplish this: decide where you are headed for your four major Sundays during February, March, and April. Also, as you can, have some sense of two other Sundays during that time. What I would *not* do is look sequentially at all thirteen weeks of February, March, and April and then try to come up with what you are going to do for a sermon each of those thirteen Sundays.

What counts are the four major Sundays and maybe two more. What happens is this. Now it is the Friday or Saturday before one of your major Sundays, say in March. You are not starting from scratch. You hit the ground running, because your ideas and preparation have been mulling in your mind since that short-term, highly intensive retreat in January.

Some excellent sprinter pastors live through many years of their ministry feeling guilty because they cannot do sermon preparation the way they were taught in seminary. Be at peace. Excellent sprinters do not do sermon preparation well that way. In the preaching seminars I do, when I share this excellent sprinter method of sermon preparation with ministers, the relief floods in, the guilt is released, and a sense of joy, rather than dread, comes to these ministers' sermon preparation.

You can do three days for the coming two months. In August, you can take three days and have fun. Study, pray, think, and relax. Discover where you are headed in September and October for two major Sundays and two more. As a result, you will know where you are headed for four out of the eight Sundays. God will bless the other Sundays too.

When you have the confidence of knowing where you are headed on your major Sundays and on two more Sundays, the spillover effects on the other Sundays are amazing.

This is the method of preparation I commend to excellent sprinters. You will tailor the method to your own way of doing preparation. The basic principle is helpful. It works. What works less well is *not* doing this and then coming to Friday and having to try to come up with something from scratch.

Let's look at an example. Each January, Tom, an excellent sprinter, uses four days of sermon preparation for the coming three months. He discovers where he is headed on his four major Sundays, and he has some sense of where he is headed on two other Sundays. He does not come back from four days of retreat knowing every text, every theme, every topic, and the outline for each sermon for thirteen weeks. That is not how sprinters do life. What does Tom do with the other seven Sundays in the three months?

He has the confidence of knowing where he is headed on his four major Sundays and two more. Further, he has the confidence that the other seven Sundays will come along. He is at peace. He does not allow himself to become preoccupied with details for all thirteen weeks. He has learned that when he does that, he develops a mental block. His mind freezes. His heart closes. Analysis-paralysis sets in. Perfectionism shows up. Complexity joins in. Nothing comes.

Tom has fun with four major sermons and two others. His few days of intensive preparation for the coming three months are well done. Then he feels free in a given week to do as he has usually done: begin his sermon preparation on Friday or Saturday.

Tom takes four days in April for May, June, and July. He does the same in July for August, September, and October. He finds four days in October for November, December, and January. His pattern varies from year to year, depending on when he takes his vacation, which he tends to spread out over the year rather than take all in one month. You will find a pattern that works for you. Countless ministers have discovered the value and benefits of this excellent sprinter method of preparation.

You have noticed that I have not suggested that sprinters go off and plan all their sermons for the coming six months. I have friends—marathon runners—who take the month of July and plan their preaching for the whole year. They do this well. If you are a marathon runner you might try that, but it is not everybody's way of doing it. For excellent sprinters, the art is to discover several short-term, highly intensive times of preparation during the year, using four days each time to look three months ahead.

Marathon Preparation

For those of us who have learned how to be solid marathon runners, our sermon preparation looks something like this:

Monday, we study the Scripture, consult the commentaries, begin to develop the exegesis, and track out the references related to the text.

Tuesday, we develop the sermon outline and the beginning of the illustrations, develop point one, and further consult the commentaries.

Wednesday, we have fun developing points two and three, when it is a three-point sermon. We begin our first draft of the sermon and develop further references.

Thursday, we develop draft two of the sermon, improve the illustrations, and do a little more work with the commentaries and references.

Friday, we do any final work with the references, develop the final draft of the sermon, find the closing illustration that is fitting, and practice the sermon.

I have good friends who are ministers all over this planet who, week by week, use this method of sermon preparation consistently and well. To be sure, there are variations on this method. The spirit of the method is to work consistently and regularly each day on the sermon for the coming Sunday.

Most courses in homiletics have taught students that this is the way to prepare. One reason homiletics courses teach people to prepare this way is that most such courses are taught in seminaries. Seminaries are solid marathon runner environments. Among seminary professors, there is a high density of solid marathon runners. It usually takes being a solid marathon runner to earn the Ph.D. to teach in the seminary.

A Sense of Balance

The more balance in your preparation, the more helpful your preaching will be. To think this through, imagine a spectrum: *simple, stirring, inspiring,* and *emotional* on one end, *complex, thoughtful, profound,* and *intellectual* on the other.

We are emotional beings. We hear a sermon hoping that our deepest longings, yearnings, and aspirations will be stirred and inspired. We look for sermons that touch our hearts. We are also intellectual beings. We listen to a sermon hoping that our understanding of everyday, ordinary life, in the light of the Gospel, will be thoughtfully and profoundly deepened. We look for sermons that touch our minds.

Some sermons touch the whole person with the whole Gospel through the whole sermon. They have a sense of balance. Some sermons stir our hearts. Some deepen our minds. Some sermons are motivational. Some are teaching. To be all motivational or all teaching would be out of balance. Over the course of several Sundays, the art is balance.

Sometimes, in our eagerness to do well, we overprepare a sermon. Our approach to sermon preparation is complex, with considerable research, much reading, and many sources. The result is a complex sermon with numerous quotations, many intricate side points, and a vocabulary of fifty-dollar and hundred-dollar words. Such a sermon does not motivate people to grow forward their lives. Indeed, it is likely too complex as a teaching sermon. The art is to do enough preparation that you have a helpful sermon, but not so much preparation that the sermon becomes too complex.

A key principle in life is this: *seek progress, not perfection.* Ministers who bring a compulsion toward perfectionism to their lives bring the same compulsion to their preaching, which I think is one reason why so many complex sermons show up. I encourage you to bring a spirit of progress, rather than perfectionism, to your sermon preparation.

The art, finally, is balance. Feel free to be at various places on the spectrum from Sunday to Sunday. Some weeks, feel free to have a simple way of preparing; be confident of having a sermon that is on the simple, stirring, inspiring end of the spectrum. For Christmas, keep it simple. For Easter, keep it simple. On your major Sundays, keep it simple. If on some other Sundays your preparation and your sermon are more complex, that's fine.

Preparation, done with simplicity, creates a sermon that, with simplicity, helps people discover the grace of God. On the major Sundays we sometimes try too hard: the sermon preparation is too complex, we are trying to hit too many home runs, and our sermons end up delivering advanced trigonometry when what helps, especially on the major Sundays, is basic math. The simpler the preparation, the simpler the sermon—and the more helpful the sermon. There is a direct correlation between how people prepare and the content they share.

How one feels during the preparation shapes how one preaches. Sometimes, as we prepare a sermon, we sense we are surrounded by the grace of God. What shows up on Sunday is a sermon of grace. Sometimes we experience tension and anxiety during our sermon preparation. What results from that is a tense, tight, nervous, anxious sermon.

When someone is depressed during the preparation, what shows up on Sunday is a depressing sermon. Sometimes, for a variety of reasons, we are angry during sermon preparation. What shows up on Sunday is an angry sermon—usually under the guise of a sermon on commitment. The direct correlation shows up.

How we prepare and how we feel during the preparation shape how we preach. When the preparation has about it the quality of simplicity, what shows up on Sunday mornings are simple, stirring, inspiring sermons that help people discover the grace of God. When sermon preparation has balance, what shows up are sermons that, over the course of several Sundays, with balance lead people to the grace of God.

Where You Prepare

The place where you prepare shapes the sermon you share. The place where you prepare your sermon shapes what you say. The physical location, the environment with which you surround yourself, shapes the results you achieve. Discover the place that helps you have fun preparing your sermons.

For example, some ministers prepare their sermons in a "designated preaching place," a study set aside for sermon preparation. What emerge are sermons of compassion and community. Regrettably, some ministers prepare their sermons in what is mostly an administrative office space, and the sermons that emerge, week after week, are sermons that focus on the institution and organization.

Some ministers prepare their sermons in a community place, such as a quiet corner in a family-run restaurant. What emerge are sermons with a spirit of community. In good weather, some ministers prepare their sermons in a park. What emerge are sermons of wonder and joy, helpfulness and hope.

For your preparation, pick a place you associate with good fun and good times. You are probably used to working at a desk that has at least one stack of papers there, probably more. When you get two stacks of paper side by side, they begin to multiply. I see many desks stacked high with piles and piles of paper.

I've always expected one of the religious publishing houses to come out with a little miniature bulldozer designed for pastors. You could give it as a gift to a beloved pastor. You could get it in the liturgical color of your choice. You could get any one of the disciples in the driver's seat. Battery operated and rechargeable, it would be designed for the pastor to use on his or her desk.

The pastor would set the bulldozer on the desk, turn on the switch, and the bulldozer would push and shove, push and shove the stacks of paper around so that for perhaps the first time in years, the pastor could see the level surface of the desk. It is not true that pastors have poor handwriting; it simply is hard to write up and down on the stacks on the desk.

My bulldozer idea is a slight overstatement made in the spirit of good fun, but nevertheless I see lots of administrative desks, piled high with papers, that, regrettably, are used as the place to prepare sermons.

Two problems emerge. First, the stacks of paperwork encourage distraction. The mind wanders well enough on its own, without further assistance. Give the mind all this mess of papers to start with, and distraction accelerates.

Second, the stacks of paper represent lots of unfinished projects. If they were finished, the papers would not be on the desk. The pastor's mind wanders to this unfinished project or that as yet incomplete business. Stacks of unfinished projects generate a deepening of depression. There are enough unfinished projects on many of our desks for anyone to get depressed!

What happens when people feel an acceleration of distraction is that they *challenge* themselves to the project at hand. People who feel a deepening of depression assume they need to develop more *commitment*. Thus, what shows up Sunday after Sunday are sermons of challenge and commitment, rather than the messages of grace and hope, compassion, and community that your people long for and need. (I discuss this subject further in Chapter Six.)

Instead of preparing your sermon at your administrative desk, I encourage you to search out any working surface and have on that surface only the pieces of paper necessary to the task at hand, namely, the preparation of this sermon. The working surface could be a table in a quiet corner of a friendly restaurant, or a desk in a Sunday school classroom, or a work surface in a community place.

Two things will now happen. First, you will have a sense of direction. Your focus will be on the sermon. Second, you will have a sense of development. What will show up are sermons that have about them a sense of compassion and a spirit of community. The *place* of preparation shapes the preaching.

In some pastors' offices there is an "administrative desk," where the piles and stacks of paper are. For sermon preparation, there is another work surface. It may be behind or beside the desk, in an alcove or in a separate space. It can be a study that has a window and in which the minister gathers mementos that remind him or her of good fun and good times. There are no filing cabinets. There may be a computer. For some, the computer functions as the work surface cleared of clutter. It becomes the single-focus, single-action work surface for sermon preparation. Somewhere in that office we want a simple surface.

Time management teaches us the "clear desk" principle: when you work on a clear desk you can produce the same amount of excellent work in one-third less time. If you are investing fifteen hours a weeks in sermon preparation on a cluttered administrative desk, then on a clear work surface you will produce the same helpful sermon in ten hours. But the "clear desk" principle is not the point here.

I am not proposing that we clear off our desks. Please do not do that. These stacks have been with us a long time. They have their own names. They are part of the family. What I am proposing is this: preparing sermons at an administrative desk creates sermons of challenge and commitment—institutional sermons.

Find any other working surface—you could even use an ironing board—where you have your Bible and the few pieces of paper necessary for the sermon at hand. What will show up on Sunday is a *helpful* sermon. Where we prepare our sermons shapes what we preach.

Shepherding

Where we invest our time shapes what and how we preach. The more shepherding, the more helpful the preaching. The less shepherding, the less helpful the preaching. The more time we invest in administration, the more likely the result will be a more institutional type of preaching. Likewise, the more time we invest in shepherding, the more the result will be a helpful, pastoral type of preaching.

As a church grows 100 percent in worship attendance, the administrative load increases 100 percent. What is also true is that, when the worship attendance grows by 100 percent, the shepherding load grows by 300 percent.

One of the reasons some churches get stuck on a plateau is that the inspiration for their growth—namely, their shepherding—falls away when the shepherd becomes preoccupied with administration. When the shepherd quits doing what she does well, she loses the chance to shepherd this greater number of people.

Three hundred percent is a conservative estimate. Years ago, in one congregation where Julie and I served, which had a strong mission with people wrestling with alcoholism, when we helped one alcoholic, he would bring us five more of his friends to help. There was literally a 500 percent increase in shepherding. Fortunately, two or three of the five helped eventually became part of the helping team. The new helpers came from among the people who were helped in the mission.

It is not necessarily true that as a church grows, the shepherd needs to learn how to become a sheep rancher. As a church grows, it is important that the shepherd gather some or all of the following persons on the staff team:

- Administrative assistant or executive secretary
- Program development director
- Specific program staff
- Church administrator

Together, this team knows how to do the "ranching." The secretarial work, the financial, property, office, and personnel administration, the programs, and the giving development move forward.

Many good shepherds are "off their game" when they try to become sheep ranchers. If your gift is shepherding, gather around you a staff of people who know how to do the ranching. The more administration you do, the more institutional your preaching will be.

Delegating work effectively has to do with trust. As pastors we can learn how to trust people who can do administrative work quicker, faster, and better than we do it. Would you go to a doctor who is on the phone making her own appointments? You would wonder why the doctor has so much free time. Excellent doctors trust others on their team to handle the administration. Excellent pastors do the same. This trust in others to do the administration frees both doctors and pastors to invest their time with people.

In shepherding, we discover the ways in which people are living whole, healthy lives. We learn how they live everyday, ordinary life. We help them in times of births and deaths. We help people with tragic events and sinful events. We are with them in celebratory events. We share with people in hope-fulfilling events.

In shepherding, we discover what is happening in people's lives. We discover health and sickness, celebration and tragedy, hope and future. We cannot discover these components of living in committee meetings, paperwork, or administrative detail.

I am for administration. I encourage you to invest a reasonable, thoughtful amount of time in administration. I lead seminars on leadership, administration, and giving development to help ministers, staff, and leaders in these areas. I founded the National Certification Program in Church Finance and Administration thirty-plus years ago precisely to help ministers and church administrators advance their competencies in administration. This program, copied in many parts of the country, has trained and certified most of the church administrators who are currently practicing. The reason I founded the program was to build a network of people who know how to do church administration well so that pastors could be about their shepherding.

Your relationship with your people shapes how ready they are to hear what you share in your sermon. Helpful preaching is partly the sermon itself and partly how well disposed people are to hear you. The closer your relationship with your people, the more ready they are to hear the wisdom and help in your sermon.

Consider two pastors whose preaching could objectively be rated 7 on a scale of 1 to 10. One pastor is a good shepherd. He has a close, rich, full relationship with his people. His congregation hears his preaching as a 9. The other pastor is not a good shepherd. His congregation hears his preaching as a 5. It is a lot more fun to be ranked as a 9 than as a 5. The congregation's openness and readiness to hear the sermon are direct results of the shepherding the members have experienced.

One of the large churches in this country was built under the leadership of a pastor who virtually mumbles and mutters his sermons. You and I would probably rate his sermon as a 3 on a scale of 1 to 10. He is legendary as a good shepherd in the community. His people gather on Sunday to hear the wisdom and compassion of their good shepherd, and whereas we might rate the sermon as a 3, they perceive the sermon as a solid 10. It is within the context of shepherding that people hear the sermon.

Shepherding is a wonderful form of sermon preparation. It is in the shepherding that you discover what is stirring in people's lives. When you are purposely shepherding, you are also doing your sermon preparation. Count your shepherding as part of the hours of sermon preparation you are doing. Literally, count these hours. Sometimes I suggest that pastors invest one hour in shepherding for each minute they preach.

During the coming year, select a number of persons you will have fun intentionally shepherding. You can purposely pick, for example, thirty-five persons. Fifteen can be persons in the community you serve in mission. Ten can be constituents who participate in some program or activity in your church. Ten can be members of your congregation. Have fun intentionally shepherding these people. During the year, in a one-time shepherding visit, seek them out. Intentionally share the grace of your shepherding with them.

I suggest a slightly higher number of community persons than members because all healthy movements grow forward more in the community than in the church. Jesus was in the community; Francis was in the community; Luther was in the community; Wesley was in the community; Booth was in the community. People who do most of their shepherding inside the church tend to preach "inside-the-church" sermons. People who invest some of their shepherding with persons in the community create sermons that are helpful with the whole community.

Often, our shepherding is reactive—something happens, and we go. I am inviting you to a proactive process. Pick a number of people you would have fun shepherding and seek them out. Gently, compassionately, share with them the grace and compassion of your shepherding. What will happen is that your preaching will grow an even richer sense of grace and compassion.

There was a principle we were taught: "Spend one hour in preparation for each minute you preach." That principle confirms the importance of sermon preparation. So do I. That principle worked well in a time when four things were true. One, it was a churched culture. Two, it was "the thing to do" to go to church, and people were seeking out the church of their own volition. Three, there was a large, multiperson staff to do much of the work. Four, the pastor's sermons were intended to be printed in books; helpful, yes, and published. Even in that time, one of the great preachers of that day once said that he quit shepherding for several months and almost ran out of anything on which to preach.

Four things are true in our time. One, we live in one of the greatest ages for mission the Christian movement has ever known. Two, we, in the name of the grace of God, will seek people out, rather than wait on them to find us. Three—and this is the case in most congregations—there is not a large, multiperson staff to do much of the work. Four, the purpose of the preaching is to be helpful in people's lives, not necessarily to be printed and published in books.

Ministers do their sermon preparation both in their shepherding and in their study. One way to think of this principle is to spend one hour in preparation for each minute you preach, and count the hours you spend in shepherding as part of your sermon preparation. Technically, I don't literally mean "one hour, one minute." What I mean is that on a mission field it's the shepherding that helps deliver the preaching. Indeed, I think this was true in a churched culture as well.

Spend some of your sermon preparation in your study. Spend some of your sermon preparation in your shepherding. When you are shepherding, you are doing sermon preparation. See your study and your shepherding as good friends in advancing your preaching. God will bless your preaching.

Three Suggestions

First, as best you can, develop a competent team of volunteers and part-time and full-time staff persons who give leadership to much of the mission and work of your congregation. When there is not enough staff support available to you, you may have a tendency to drift toward or become preoccupied with administration. The key is to discover several key leaders, volunteers, and staff who can help with some of it.

When they do it well, share "Well done" and "Thank you" with them. When they do not do so well, be at peace. Do not allow yourself to be drawn in to doing it for them. Give them the chance to learn from their excellent mistakes. Share with them your wisdom and experience, your encouragement and coaching.

Wherever the preaching is helpful, I usually find a team of competent, compassionate volunteers, part-time and full-time staff, or some combination thereof, who free the pastor to focus on sermon preparation. I teach congregations to put in place such a team so as to help advance the preaching. And the preaching does advance.

Second, each day, practice the "20-80" principle: 20 percent of the things a person or group does delivers 80 percent of their results, accomplishments, and achievements. Especially when you do not have sufficient staff support, it is important to focus on the "20 percenter" objectives that deliver 80 percent of the results.

Do not get caught up in inconsequential issues, such as whether to have blue or yellow name tags at a covered-dish supper, or where the kitchen utensils are stored, or the appropriate location to keep a certain table used twice a year. Focus on progress and, as best you can, keep in check any tendency to become compulsive about perfection.

Regrettably, we sometimes allow ourselves to be distracted from our sermon preparation by negligible, almost insignificant matters. Some of these administrative issues can "drop through the cracks" with modest or no significant loss. It's more important that some of the people you serve in mission avoid falling through the cracks in their lives. Your sermons of grace are decisive.

Sometimes we do not have the choice of keeping everything from dropping through the cracks. The choice is, Where do I focus my energies: people and shepherding, or administration? Administration is the less crucial of the two. When I work with congregations caught on a plateau, what I find, mostly, is that these congregations have quit doing the things they once did well, the things that had to do with the shepherding and that enriched the preaching. They have gotten caught in administration. The shepherding and the preaching have suffered as a consequence.

Third, the art of advancing your sermon preparation is to pick one of these four areas: method, balance, place, or shepherding. Have fun growing this one. Later, pick another one of the four and have fun developing it. Some ministers say, "I want to work on all four of these." I encourage you to maintain a pace of working on *one* this year. Develop *one* next year. Save some for future years. When you get two of these four up and running, the other two will come along on their own. As you advance your sermon preparation, your preaching will become even more helpful in people's lives.

4

Resources

How you resource your preaching shapes how and what you preach. By letting people teach you, you will strengthen your preaching. You, your key leaders, and the grassroots people in your congregation and in your community can have fun and help you advance your preaching by discovering resources together.

In one sense, resources are the things we have—our material possessions, financial assets, property, belongings, supplies, products, and the stuff we own. In a fuller sense, the resources God gives us are the *people* with whom we live this life through. God gives us our family, our friends, our key leaders and the grassroots of our congregation, and the people in our community and across the planet. Their strengths, gifts, and competencies enrich our lives. Their wisdom and experience, their excellent ideas and good suggestions, their longings and hopes, their spirit of compassion, and their sense of community strengthen our lives and resource our preaching.

You can develop resources for your preaching by participating in a

- Research team
- Community group
- Bible study group
- Prayer team
- Preaching group

Research Team

This is your team. Corporately, supportively, your research team brings you a rich array of materials for the sermons designed for *this* specific congregation, in *this* distinctive community, at *this* particular time. This excellent sprinter team delivers resources and discoveries that you then do not have to find all by yourself. They look for insights that contribute to the helpfulness and strength of the message on a given Sunday morning.

They deliver both their own wisdom and the wisdom they locate as they research on your behalf. They discover clues that help people develop a whole, healthy life. They detect almost the beginnings of an idea that lead people forward. They discover words, phrases, and sentences that share these ideas succinctly, helpfully, memorably. They hit upon illustrations that complement and help interpret the message of the morning. They find analogies, stories, and parables that advance how this sermon can helpfully unfold.

You give your research team the Scripture and the theme for the four major Sundays in the coming three months. Each person on your team knows how to explore a distinctive array of sources in their research. Their research carries them to a wide range of commentaries, journals, and CDs, to the Internet, and so on. They bring to you—quickly—the one, two, or at most three pages that will help resource your sermons.

You do not want each of your team to give you forty pages of material; you might get forty pages from one and thirty from another, and soon you end up with ninety pages. Instead, you want persons on your research team who can find thirty pages of material and distill it down to the two or three pages that help directly, specifically with a given sermon. Rather than bring you ten illustrations, they find fifteen or twenty and then bring you the best one or two that fit.

One person who serves on a research team is David. He knows his way around the resources of Scripture, biblical commentaries, sermons, prayers, devotionals, and theological and biblical journals. David has never been to seminary, yet in his own spiritual pilgrimage he has found his way to and through these resources. He brings this expertise with him to the research team. He does not know everything about the Bible, but he knows a number of biblical commentaries and journals that are helpful. He knows how to find his way through these materials and summarize them in two to three essential pages relating directly to the text. He helps greatly to advance his pastor's sermons.

Ann knows her way through the literature of life enrichment, personal and spiritual growth, family development, and stages of life. She knows a range of resources about specific human hurts and hopes. Although Ann does not know everything about all these areas, she knows how to find her way into and through them. Moreover, she knows a variety of people in the community who can point her to this resource or that suggestion, to this insight or that clue. Research is not limited to written or recorded sources. Research means visiting with people as well. Ann is connected to many helpful networks in the community.

Sharon's gifts are in drama, art, and music. Her passion is drama, and she also brings experience in art and music. She knows much of the literature in these fields. Moreover, she knows the leaders in the drama, art, and music groups in the community, and she knows how to find people in these groups who can be resources for her as she does her research.

John brings resources from educational, vocational, economic, political, governmental, and civic and community circles. His chief interest and experience is in educational and vocational research. This leads him to the other areas. Moreover, he can find wisdom on trends emerging in the community and in the culture.

These are four gifted, helpful people. David, Ann, Sharon, and John complement each other in terms of the networks of people and literature they bring to a research team. There is no point in having team members who know the same areas of research. You benefit most from a team's complementary research capabilities. The richness of these four people is that they draw on the resources that have impact in people's lives and destinies in everyday, ordinary life.

In another research team, Alice was an excellent team member because she had celebrated fifteen "birthdays." She had lived fifteen years as a recovering alcoholic. She knew this world well. She had access to many groups in the community and to a wealth of wisdom and experience to share with her pastor. Her suggestions enriched and strengthened his sermons.

I want you to be thinking. You may already know someone who can bring a range of resources to your preaching. Frequently, we discover God has planted these people right in front of us. Somewhere around you is someone like David or Ann. Somewhere God has already given you Sharon, John, or Alice. Take one moment, even as you read these words, and affirm to yourself the name of one or two persons who you know would have fun being a part of your research team.

In the community there is someone—maybe not in your church—who has never been asked to be part of a solid research team, and for a short period of time that person would be happy to share with you. When you begin to think about your team, you don't have to start going through your membership list. Think about persons. You may find persons in the community who have a primary relationship with you through a common interest, a service club, or a community activity. Feel free to invite those persons to be part of your research team for a three-month excellent sprint. They'll puzzle about how they can do it, and then they'll discover they do it well.

Your research team is an excellent sprinter team, not a group of marathon runners. The team shares resources with you for a three-month period. The team can help you for as few as two months or as many as four months, but the same team will not be resourcing you for a full year. You can have one team for a given part of the year and then have another team for another part of the year.

For example, you can have a research team that resources your preaching for February, March, and April in a given year. Have a wonderful, one-time, good-fun gathering with them in January, shortly after your "four days for three months" study time (described in Chapter Three). Share with them where you are heading on the four major Sundays in that three-month period. Then turn them loose. Give them the text and theme, plus your current best thinking on these four sermons and perhaps on two more. Then let them teach you informally as they research these sermons.

You do not meet with your excellent sprinter team each week. You can have a good-fun, midpoint gathering in March. This is a time of helpful collaboration. Together you share resources that are directly helpful now and those that you will save for the future. Further, you share your wisdom about particular resources that are not helpful, that are blind alleys. Let the team members feel free to no longer look in those areas. They do not need to spend their time chasing rabbits. Discuss the possibilities you and your team hope yet to discover.

During the three months, your team has the advantage of ongoing "action learning." What you use for a sermon teaches the team members what to look for to resource other sermons. What you do not use teaches them what not to look for. They learn what helps as they listen to your sermon on a given Sunday. They discover what you use and what you don't use. These are pros who, with these clues, are able to reshape where they look and, therefore, what they find.

When the three months have come and gone, you have a concluding session with them in early May. You thank them. You say "Well done" to them and share with them the particular kinds of resources that were directly helpful. They will thank you for the privilege of being members of a research team with you. You can visit with them about the possibility of whether some of them would have fun being your research team at some time next year.

You don't need to "lock in" this team for the next year. You may discover that two of the four people were really helpful, and, at a later time, you might invite these two to be a part of another team. You might also decide to have an entirely new team of three to four persons for February through April next year. This is your choice.

You can select several persons as a research team who work with you during May, June, and July of a given year. You can have a one-time meeting with them in April, and they provide resources for your preaching as you head to Pentecost and beyond.

Likewise, you can have another group that has fun sharing with you as a research team for October, November, and December. These three to five people meet with you, one time, in September, and they provide research for your preaching as you head to Christmas. In your one-time September gathering, share with them about the four major Sundays in October, November, and December.

Help them know the Scriptures around which you look forward to developing these four sermons. Share with them your current sense of the theme, the focus, and the direction in which you think each of these four sermons is heading. You do not need to provide them a detailed sermon outline. Give them some clue as to your best wisdom on the emerging content as you give thought and prayer to these four texts. Then turn them loose to have fun researching.

Two benefits result from having different research teams at specific times of the year. First, by having more than one team you receive a broader, richer, deeper range of resources than you would from one. Second, having a research team work with you for three months is a good pace. The team members will enjoy researching material with you using this short-term time frame, and because they are working at the pace of excellent sprinters, your sermons will tend toward being sprinters' sermons.

You see I am suggesting you avoid having a research team that works with you throughout a whole year. You could do that, but it will feel like a solid marathon runner research team. When we resource our preaching in a solid marathon manner, we tend to create solid marathon sermons Sunday after Sunday, but, as I discussed in Chapter Three, you will be delivering those sermons in an excellent sprinter culture.

Therefore I invite you to have two or three excellent sprinter teams who have fun helping you at given times of the year. Now, I am not suggesting that you have to have three research teams a year. I am suggesting that you develop more than one and do so for whatever cluster of three or four months makes sense to you. Tailor your research teams so that they directly benefit and help you with your preaching.

To be sure, those of us whose style and pace are more that of solid marathon runners actually already know the Scripture, the sermon title, and the basic outline for all thirteen of these Sundays. Those of us who are excellent sprinters will be discovering some of the nine Sundays as each of them comes to us, and we will do excellent sprints. That is fine.

You want your research team to come up with excellent ideas and good suggestions primarily for the four major Sundays. You'll be amazed at the ideas and suggestions that will come when you give your team the freedom to help you puzzle through what sermons will be helpful for the other nine Sundays. You are inviting your research team members to help you with these discoveries. Let them teach you.

A sermon is a *corporate* event between the congregation and the minister. We *together* participate in the event of the sermon. A sermon need not be a one-person project—either when it is prepared or when it is preached. We can participate together both in the preparing and the preaching. Once we understand the corporate nature of the sermon, then we can think of our research as being corporate rather than singular, team rather than individual.

Community Group

An excellent way to discover resources for your preaching is to participate in a community group whose focus is the same community God gives you as your mission field. Pick a community group with which you would have fun. Participate in the group's one-time community projects that are helpful in people's lives. You will benefit your preaching through your new discoveries, new wisdom, and new insights about how people live everyday, ordinary lives in your community in our time. Many of you are already doing this in your community.

When we spend our time primarily inside the church, our sermons tend to lack insight into the lives of everyday people. The sermons tend to be preoccupied with "stuff" inside the church. The resources for our preaching are found in our community as well as in our church.

God gives us an amazing array of community groups. Some are formal, institutional, systematic, and well organized. Some groups are more informal, relational, relaxed, and spontaneous. In recent years, there has been a modest shift from the more formal to the more informal, relational groupings. The possibilities, both formal and informal, include groups whose focus is

vocational, professional	artistic, musical
sociological, ethnic	educational
geographical	retired persons
human hurt, hope	political, governmental
life stages	recreational
civic, community	business
hobbies, interests	religious

Select one of these groups and have fun participating in a one-time project. You can pick a hobby or interest group, a political or governmental group. You can rehearse and sing with the community choir for the Fourth of July celebration, play on the summer softball team, or work on a community website project. God invites us to know and serve the *whole* community. The whole community comprises an amazing array of these groups.

For example, you may feel drawn to help with early elementary education. Consider when a school or preschool has its most difficulties and anxieties. What time of year could you offer help in a school? It is not something you are necessarily looking to do each week. During a three-month period, participate in one, one-time project.

Or your interest may be junior high school–age children. Have fun being part of a one-time, short-term, highly intensive tutoring project. Or help families in a one-time workshop that the school or some educational group is holding.

Whenever you work with or participate in any community group, you will discover

- The goals and values of the group
- The customs, habits, and traditions that are part of the group
- The language and communication network with which the group lives
- The leadership and decision-making process within the group
- The group's sacred place of meeting
- The group members' common shared vision of the future

Once you have the clue to look for these things, you usually will find them. You don't need to sit down and ask the leaders of some community group, "Teach me the goals and values of this group." Just listen and be aware, and from their conversation you will learn the goals and values of the group.

They will teach you the jargon, buzzwords, and manner of speaking with which they work. They will teach you the sacred places of meeting important to them. Most important, they will teach you their common shared vision of the future. Most often, all you have to do is say, "Share with me—tell me—about your group," and all of this will unfold.

Every community has most, if not all, of the groups mentioned previously, and some wield considerable influence and power. In one Florida community, the recreation department is among the most influential and helpful of all these groups. In one city on the West Coast, the most influential groups are the political and governmental. In some communities in Indiana, the basketball leagues are informal but influential groups.

Generally speaking, in any community, four groups tend to be the leading, most influential groups in the community. The four will vary from one community to the next. Be drawn to whatever group you would have fun with. At the same time, when you have fun with one of the four influential groups in your community, you will now have a resource for your sermons from across the whole community. When you touch one of those four, you tend to touch more of the whole community, because these four groups will be the pervasive sources of influence in the community.

Likewise, in any community, some group or groups tend to be among the least powerful groups in the community. These will vary from one community to the next. It will be helpful for you to participate, at some time, in a project that helps you come to know and understand this group. You will now have a preaching resource that helps you understand the predicament and plight of the least favored in the community. As you let the whole community enrich your preaching, your sermons will increasingly touch the whole community.

Bible Study Group

Choose a short-term, highly intensive group—an excellent sprinter group that is going to study some portion of the Scriptures together. The group has fun on a weekend retreat studying some specific texts of Scripture. Or the group meets for three to five sessions.

You can enjoy *not* being the leader of this Bible study group. You are welcome to be a participant. It helps for the group to include some new Christians and people who are exploring becoming Christians. You are welcome to have some community people. You can focus on specific Scriptures that will advance the preaching for the coming three months. This is a grassroots group.

You are welcome to be part of a Bible study group composed primarily of your long-time key leaders. Simply know this will tend to be an advanced group. They have studied the

Bible for many years. From time to time, the group may discuss "church stuff." As a group, they may tend to have an institutional focus about the church. That is what long-time key leaders often have been taught to have an interest in. A grassroots Bible study group can include a few key leaders. Mostly, the group includes a range of people who are grass roots.

The early Christians studied the Bible in one-time study groups. When a letter came from Paul, they got together and studied it. Then, on another occasion, they studied it again. They studied it another one time. In those early days, there was not enough of the New Testament gathered together to organize long-term Bible studies. It was one-time Bible study. When I talk with missionaries today across the planet, they teach me that they do many one-time Bible studies.

This is a mission field. Have a one-time retreat. Or, you can have three sessions, or as many as five. As soon as we plan six sessions, we have lost all the excellent sprinters. What we're looking for are the fresh insights you will gain as a participant with grassroots people—insights that help you bring a fresh, relevant message in your sermon.

Prayer Team

A special resource is a prayer team. Invite several persons who would have fun being a prayer team for your preaching for three months. "Henry, Mary, and Sue, I invite you to be the prayer team for the preaching that will take place in May, June, and July this year." You can choose another prayer team for another period of time.

Preaching is prayer. You can pray the sermon into being. The sermon is a sacramental prayer that lifts unto God the hopes and hurts of this community, this congregation, in light of this text.

Your team prays that people find the sermon helpful in their lives. Your team prays that people discover the grace of God in the sermon this Sunday. They pray that people find a new way of thinking about their lives—their present and their future—that they discover handles of help and hope for their lives. Your prayer team prays that people advance whole, healthy lives in relation to their family, their work, and their friends.

Your prayer team prays for you—that you relax and have fun and enjoy life and live in Christ. Your prayer team prays that you not try too hard to do too much good in one sermon. Your prayer team prays that the sermon helps you in your life. It's not just that the sermon helps the people of your congregation with their lives. As we prepare and share the sermon, it helps us with our own lives. Your prayer team prays that the sermon leads us to the meaning and hope God has for our lives.

It is amazing to have the sense that two to three people are deeply in prayer for your preaching.

Preaching Group

You can have fun participating in a short-term, highly intensive preaching group. You can meet weekly for three to five weeks, or you can have fun going off together on a retreat. You can do some fishing, some golfing, and some sitting around sharing stories, and you can help each other with your preaching. You can rotate the leader so that somebody different leads each session. You can include pastors whose gifts and strengths mutually resource one another.

You can look at specific Scriptures and discover how to advance your sermons for the four major Sundays during the coming three months. The focus of your gathering is on your preaching. A preaching group is not a support group, a counseling group, or primarily a social group. You will do some of these things, but you gather as a group to resource one another on your preaching.

Healthy Competencies

In resourcing your preaching—whether through research teams, community groups, Bible study groups, prayer teams, or preaching groups—you are looking for persons with healthy competencies for living life, who live in the grace of God. You want people who look at the whole, not the parts: the *whole* of a person's life, the *whole* of the Gospel, the *whole* of the community we are serving in mission.

You want persons who exemplify a lively spirit of compassion and a rich sense of community. You are looking for people who bring wisdom and judgment, vision and common sense, who bring profound helpfulness about life. You are looking for people who have a deep desire to help you. They have some sense of loyalty to you and to the mission you are sharing. They have insight and access into specific resource areas that help. They promptly share these resources with you.

You are not looking for the compulsive perfectionist. Nor do you want the person who brings their low self-esteem, lamenting, and complaining. Nor are you looking for persons who wallow in their problems, in a codependent-dependent fashion. You are looking for people who are living through and beyond the problems with which they are wrestling in life.

You do not need someone who is angry with the community or the church. Given the age of mission with which God blesses us, we will have our own fair share of despair, depression, and anger. These come with the human hurts and hopes around us and in us. We do not need persons resourcing us who are frequently despairing, depressed, or angry. You are looking for whole, healthy persons who are the best they can be in their own lives.

You want people who have no axe to grind—people who are not on a campaign to propose their pet project or support some theological point of view of their own. We do not need people who are trying, quietly, incessantly, to put their words into our mouths. You do not want persons who want you to preach their sermons. You are looking for people who have a sense of the spirit of the congregation and of the local community.

Ways Forward

Think through how you can benefit from these five kinds of resources to advance your preaching during the coming three years. Pick one you can have fun advancing this year. Pick two you can enjoy growing next year. You can pick one for each of the coming three years. Pick three that are a good match for you. The other two will come along. Focus on the three you will have fun doing.

Then, pick any three-month period for a year—you do not have to create a systematic plan that follows the same three-month cycle each year. You can do February, March, and April as we head to Easter. You can have fun with October, November, and December. You can do any three months that work for you.

Part of a year you could have a research team. In another year you could have a community group, a Bible study group, or a prayer team. For a given three months, the resources for your preaching can come primarily from your research team. For another three months, you can let it be a one-time community project. For yet another three months, you can draw on a Bible study group or a prayer team. At another time, you can be part of a preaching group.

I encourage you to be flexible in developing these resources to enhance your preaching. Your preaching will develop an extraordinary creativity. The more flexibility, the higher the level of creativity; the more rigidity, the lower the level of creativity. The more creatively you use these resources, the more helpful your preaching will be.

Your sermons benefit from a team effort. Let people teach you. Resources for your preaching do not have to be developed just by you, all by yourself. God plants all these resources around you. Have fun with whichever of these resources work for you. You will grow forward your preaching. People will discover the grace of God.

5

Content

Decisive events change people's lives and shape their destinies. Likewise, sermons with helpful content change people's lives and advance their destinies. Style is important in preaching. Substance is more important. People come to worship looking for, longing for, help for the week to come.

To be sure, we want help for the weeks and years that have been. But we know that what has been, has been. We know we can do two things about our past. One, we can ask God's forgiveness for our sins of commission and omission in the time gone by. Two, we can give thanks to God for the achievements and accomplishments of the past. We know we cannot change what has been.

We know we can do something with our present and our future. We come, not primarily looking back on the past, but looking to the future before us. We look for help for the time to come. We bring with us our anticipations and anxieties, our fears and longings, our expectancies and hopes.

You can grow forward the content of your sermons by

- Developing the message of the Scripture
- Advancing some single aspect of living
- Nurturing a person's foundational life searches
- Helping people deal with the major cultural shifts of our time

The Message of the Scripture

The art of content resides in developing the message of the Scripture. The content of the sermon is helpful when the message is grounded in and emerges from Scripture. In a helpful sermon, the scriptural basis of the sermon is simply and profoundly shared. Through that sharing, the congregation discovers handles for living. People discover the grace of God for loving one another and for sharing hope with each other in everyday, ordinary life.

Scripture is central. Professionalism and polish count for something. Meaning and content count for everything. The style and shape of a sentence are things of beauty. The help and hope of the good news are the breath of life.

Yes, it is helpful for the content of the sermon to be communicated in prose that is grammatically correct. It is even more helpful for the content of the sermon to help persons advance their lives and shape their destinies in the light of the Scripture. Invest some of your time in developing prose and polish. Invest much of your time in puzzling through how you can communicate the message of the Scriptures.

When you are studying the scriptural text for your sermon, you can ask yourself two searching questions. The first is, What does this text say? This question affirms that the text can speak to us. Yes, we bring to the text our fair share of presuppositions and prejudices. We do not come to the Scripture as a blank slate on which the text writes its meaning. We bring to the text our wisdom and experience, our current understanding of life, our fears and hopes.

The first question—What does this text say?—invites us to open ourselves to the grace and compassion, wisdom and hope in the text itself. We can let the text speak to us and teach us about the grace of God. We can allow the text to share its new life with us.

It is not so much that we suspend our wisdom and experience, nor that we set aside our current understanding of life. It is not that we become passively objective, as if that were possible or even desirable. It is not that we become inert and immobile before the text. It is more like this: we come to the text with a passion to learn from the text. We look forward to a rich interaction between our current way of looking at life and the message of the text. We bring an enthusiasm and expectancy to the Scripture. We bring a deep, abiding excitement that we will find new insights and fresh discoveries in the text that will help us advance our understanding of life and our capacity to live life well in the grace of God. With a persistent, proactive spirit, we search for the meaning in the text.

The second question we ask is, What does this text not say? This question invites us to discover the full richness and implications of the text. Know this: the text is as intentional in what it does not say as in what it does say. As you study and pray over the text, look for what the text is not saying. Your sermons will be richer and fuller for doing so.

In conversations with people, we learn as much by what people do not say as by what they do say. For example, I was visiting with a couple in our congregation. They have two children. In our talk together, the couple went on and on about all the accomplishments and achievements of their son. They briefly mentioned their daughter, but, having acknowledged her existence, they moved on to focus the whole of their conversation on their son. I learned much about the dynamics of that family by what was not said about their daughter. In visiting with people, listen as much for what is not said as for what is said.

The same is true of Scripture. For example, in Revelations 21:5 we discover these words: "And God who sat upon the throne said, 'Behold, I make all things new.'" The text affirms that God makes all things new. When we look closely for what the text does not say, we discover important insights into the way in which God relates to us.

The text does not say, "And behold, I make all things old." God does not live in the past. God does not encourage us to live in the past. God has acted quietly and lovingly, mightily and decisively, compassionately and encouragingly in the past. But God does not stay in the past. The most decisive understanding of God in the Old Testament is of the God who goes before the people, as a cloud by day and a fire by night, leading us to that future which God has promised and is preparing for us.

The text does not say, "And behold, I make all things the same." It is not true that nothing ever changes. It is not true that we cannot ever really change. Yes, old habits die hard, but they do die. We do become new persons in Christ. The most decisive understanding of God in the New Testament is of the open tomb, the risen Lord, and new life in Christ. God invites us to live beyond what now is. God invites us to a new life.

The text does not say "You [or We] make all things new." God does not leave us to our own devices and struggles. We are not in this alone, all by ourselves. God gives us the gifts and competencies to live whole, healthy lives. God gives us strengths sufficient for the time at hand. The grace of God, the compassion of Christ, and the healing hope of the Holy Spirit are with us. The promise of the gospel is that God is making all things new in your life this very moment.

Another example is in the Gospel of Luke. There, we discover the parable of the prodigal son. I call it the parable of the loving father. The key to the parable is not simply what the son did. He went to the far country, lost his inheritance, and finally gathered himself up to come home. The key is also what we learn of the father.

What the text *does not* say is, "While the young son was yet a long way off, his father saw him, and he waited in the house for his son to draw near." What the text *does not* say is, "The father remembered their last, bitter parting. He remembered having heard that his son had lost his inheritance in the far country. He remembered his own grudges and feelings of resentment and bitterness, and so he waited in the house until his son drew nigh."

The text is quite clear. "While the young son was yet a long way off, his father saw him and had compassion and he ran to him." We learn from what the text does not say. We learn that compassion does not wait; compassion runs. We learn that God does not wait for us. While we are yet a long way off, God runs to us with compassion and welcomes us home.

Fortunately, in our time, there is a wealth of commentaries and books to serve as resources in our study of the Scripture. We have available the possibilities of research teams, Bible study groups, and conversations with ministers, key leaders, and grassroots people to enrich our discovery of the meaning of the text. We have the major resource of prayer. We pray that we can open ourselves to understanding what the text is saying and what it is not saying. We approach the text in a prayerful spirit—in an almost sacramental spirit.

Words count. Words change lives. The art is to study the text in a spirit of humility, compassion, and hope. Guard against too quickly superimposing a preconceived idea. Be open to what the text is seeking to teach you. Be open to a new message about the meaning of life. Be open to the grace of God, the compassion of Christ, and the healing hope of the Holy Spirit.

Some Single Aspect of Living

The art of content is for the sermon to have a single focus—to advance some single aspect of living. This singular focus invites people to a single action that helps them advance their lives. People grow forward their lives one step at a time, one day at a time.

A sermon that has focus is rich and full in content. It is stirring and inspiring. It delivers help and hope. The sermon that tries to help everybody with everything ends up helping "nobody with nothing." It creates the mediocre middle across the board. It tries to do too much and ends up doing too little. Ask yourself, as you pray and prepare a sermon, With what single aspect of living will this sermon help people?

Content does not mean "more." Content means focus. It is not helpful for the sermon's content to try to teach people about too many areas of living in one sermon. A sermon with multiple foci, inviting people to multiple actions, is confusing and busy. It becomes too cluttered, too crowded, and too complex.

Such a sermon creates the sense that there are too many goals, those goals are set too high, and they all need to be accomplished too soon. Faced with this predicament, people tend to postpone action. You may have people who think they have a problem with procrastination. Procrastination is not the problem—it is the symptom. The root problem is a compulsion toward perfectionism. This is a learned behavior pattern, and when people allow that "old friend" to hold sway in their lives, they do set too many goals, too high, to be achieved too soon. They postpone action to postpone failure. They innately know they have set themselves up to fail. The way to not fail is to do nothing.

Sometimes, in creating a sermon, this same compulsion influences our sermon preparation. It is not accidental that we show up on a given Sunday with a sermon that tries to do too much. In our desire to be helpful, we have allowed our own compulsion to influence the sermon too much. The sermon ends up without the clear-cut singleness of focus.

Remember what it is like when you are driving down the highway and you see a sign in the distance. As you approach and pass by, the sign has a few key words. The sign is clear and uncluttered. You can read the message. You know the direction ahead. You move forward.

Further down the highway, you approach and pass by another sign. It has many words and instructions, with long sentences and tedious wording. Do you slow down or stop your car in order to read all the words? Not likely.

What happens when we realize we cannot read the whole sign? We read none of it. That is simply human nature. The sign looks too crowded and cluttered. We move on, simply looking ahead; we watch for a sign that is clearer and easier to apply to our lives.

It's like that for the members of a congregation as the members listen to a sermon. It is not accidental that the old joke about the young minister delivering "the whole bale of hay" persists. Too many foci—too many areas, too many directions—and people lose track, lose concentration, lose interest, and tune us out. We hope they will return and give us another chance to share a sermon that is singular and immediate, that they can apply directly to their lives now.

For example, my book *Twelve Keys for Living* provides people with twelve possibilities for growing a whole, healthy life. The book encourages people to claim their current strengths. Then it encourages people to select one current strength they look forward to expanding. The art is to build on our strengths, to do better what we do best. Then the book encourages people to add one new strength in their lives, to do so with a sense of progress and pace, one step at a time.

If you should choose to draw on the book, I encourage you not to build a single sermon describing, in detail, all twelve keys. You can share a sermon on any one of the twelve:

mission, compassion, hope, community, leadership, simplicity, joy, wisdom, encouragement, creativity, health, and generosity.

You might develop a single sermon briefly outlining the twelve. In general, I would focus on one of the twelve, inviting people to grow that strength in their lives. The single focus of your sermon will encourage people to a single action that will advance their lives.

The book will stir your thinking. You will discover further possibilities beyond the twelve in the book. Share them, one at a time, in your sermons. I encourage you not to allow your enthusiasm for your new discoveries to carry you away and lead you to create sermons that invite people to do too much, too soon. That, regrettably, will stir their own compulsion toward perfectionism. Focus your content.

Most often, people grow full, happy lives as they wrestle with a single focus, a single way to improve their lives. One at a time. One day at a time. The art of content is to keep it simple, with a single focus that leads people to a single life-changing action. They can thus grow and develop, advance and improve their lives in the grace of God.

Foundational Life Searches

A sermon's content can be measured by how much it helps people with their foundational life searches. Helpful preaching coaches people so that they can grow in their life searches. Its results are seen as people discover handles to grasp and use as they advance and develop in this life's pilgrimage.

The foundational life searches with which we all wrestle are the searches for

- Individuality
- Community

- Meaning
- Hope

You will find a full chapter on each of these in my book *Effective Church Leadership*, and I commend the book to you.

For our purposes now, I want simply to confirm that we live out our search for individuality as we search for identity, integrity, autonomy, and power. The search for community is our search for roots, place, belonging, and family. Our search for meaning is lived out as we search for purpose, value, and significance in our lives. Through this search, we find that our lives count, in enduring ways. We search for hope. We look for sources of hope in the present, the immediate future, the distant future, and the next-life future. We live on hope. The foundational life search for hope is central to our pilgrimage in this life.

In advancing your preaching, one step forward is for you to decide which of these foundational life searches is most helpful to *you* at this time in your own life. Do not look first at your congregation. Look at yourself. Discern, consciously, which of these searches is stirring in you now. To be sure, all four are present. Usually, one of the four is predominant at a given point in life. Life is a search. Life is a pilgrimage. At yet another point in life, it will be another one of the four. Part of the art of preaching is to develop some understanding of your own pilgrimage.

Further, you can seek to understand the predominant life search important to a *loved one in your family.* You can discover the predominant life searches important to two or three *significant relational groupings in your congregation.* Look in the *groups in your community.* As you discern which of these searches is stirring in you and in those around you, your preaching will become even more intentionally helpful.

As you prepare your next sermon, ask yourself which of these four foundational life searches this sermon will help people advance in the week to come. Ask yourself, Does where I am headed with this sermon match what is stirring now in the people with whom I am preaching?

The Major Cultural Shifts of Our Time

The content of preaching helps people deal with the major cultural shifts and trends of our time—indeed the major shifts and trends of any time. These trends directly relate to the twelve keys for living and the four foundational life searches. These shifts are powerful precisely because they *do* relate. Your sermon content can give guidance and help to your people who are faced with these sometimes beneficial, sometimes unsettling changes.

In prior years it was fashionable and, indeed, appropriate to speak of a paradigm shift—a shift or change from one worldview or one pattern of behavior to another. An accepted way of understanding life was giving way to a different worldview.

We live, now, in what I call a megadigm time, a time when multiple paradigm shifts are occurring. The term *megadigm* is intended to describe the dynamic, escalating, convoluted developments of our time. Humankind is moving through four concomitant, extraordinary, interacting shifts:

1. The shift to an informational culture
2. The shift to an excellent sprinter culture
3. The shift to a movement way of viewing life
4. The shift to living in the midst of the stars and space, to living among galaxies

These shifts—these changes—are affecting the people in your congregation. Most of us become anxious, sometimes fearful, in the midst of change. We are surrounded by disruption upon disruption, as these changes become manifest in our lives. The opportunity is here, the need is here, for you to share help through your sermon messages.

The first of these shifts is that we are currently moving away from an industrial economy toward an informational, technological economy. Many of the more economically advanced nations are undergoing this shift. In some parts of the planet, people are just now moving from a nomadic way of life to an agrarian way of life. In other places, the current shift is from an agrarian culture to an industrial way of life.

Many of your people have found that the world is no longer the familiar place with which they were comfortable. It can be frightening to face a strange, new world, a world in which it seems that the old trusted principles no longer work. This is a time for preaching that lives in a technological, informational world and that does so with an invitational spirit.

Another significant shift is that our culture is now an excellent sprinter culture, as I discussed in earlier chapters. In this time, our culture values the pace of an excellent sprinter. Where once the marathon runner's persistent, steady long-term effort was esteemed, now the culture's goals and values, the culture's positive reinforcement and rewards, encourage a sprinter's way of life—a life of short-term, highly intensive action near the time at hand.

The nomadic culture of an earlier time was a solid marathon culture. Yes, there were occasional sprints, but the routine of life was to follow the seasons, the water, and the herds. The agrarian culture was a marathon culture. There were two sprints a year: planting and harvest. Nevertheless, the years were lived out in a steady, regular, routine manner. The industrial culture was a solid marathon culture. There might be a peak-season sprint of production near Christmas, but, mostly, we were producing x number of products per day, per week, per month, year in and year out.

This is a remarkable time in the history of human civilization. The culture has shifted from a marathon way of living to a sprinter way of life. This is a major, earthquake shift, and it is not simply that we are busier now. People were busy in those earlier marathon cultures too. They were busy running several marathons at once. Their sense of busyness and their frustrations were pervasive in their lives, but the pace of their business was that of several marathon runs. The pace is now that of excellent sprints. Most important, the culture, which used to reinforce the values of a marathon culture, now positively reinforces the values of a sprinter culture.

Look anew at the story of the tortoise and the hare, a story invented in a solid marathon runner culture. Who wins? The tortoise. The story led us to devalue the speed and quickness of the hare; we have been taught that somewhere along the way the hare would slow down—even take a nap—and who knows when it would come back to finish the race? The hare would let us down. The plodding tortoise's steady forward motion—the pace of the marathon runner—was most valued.

These days, the hare wins. As never before, humankind has adopted a swifter pace of living. Life is lived in short-term, highly intensive sprints near the time at hand. Our recognition of this emerging trend invites us to rethink the customs and habits that grew up around preaching as it was in a marathon culture. This is the time of excellent sprinter preaching.

The third concomitant change is the shift from an institutional understanding of life to a movement understanding of life—from a hierarchical, empire way of life to a grassroots, clan way of life. The Egyptian, Greek, Roman, Mongolian, Holy Roman, Chinese, British, Communist worlds—all these and many more are examples of an institutional, hierarchical understanding of life. All these have made their mark, but the empires are dead.

These two paradigms—movement and institution—have been in dialogue with one another across the history of humankind. Sometimes the movement understanding of living has been predominant. Sometimes the institutional way of living has been dominant. Until very recently, the institutional understanding of life has held sway.

But in our time, people are drawn to an understanding of life—to a way of living—that is more relational, informal, relaxed, spontaneous, casual, and flexible. They are less drawn to an institutional way of life that is more functional, formal, systemic, organized, and rigid. The institutional way of living has little compelling value to most people in our time. They are drawn to a grassroots worldview, not a hierarchical worldview. The spirit of freedom that is more fully present in various places and peoples across the planet encourages a grassroots movement understanding of living. Whenever the fresh, living spirit of freedom grows, grassroots movements flourish.

In our time, helpful preaching is at the grassroots level; it does not move from the top down. It is part of a movement more than an institution, part of the community more than part of an organization.

The fourth major shift is that we now live among the stars. We now perceive that we live in the midst of space, galaxies, and solar systems unending. This is the most expansive and powerful of the four major shifts.

The older worldviews—nomadic, agrarian, and industrial—had their focus primarily on this planet. Those worldviews were "looking out" from this planet to the stars. The underlying assumptions were—and we have slowly retreated from one to the next—that this planet, this sun, this solar system, or, at least, this galaxy was somehow the center of the universe. This way of viewing life, this looking out, is giving way to an intergalactic worldview. In a way that humankind has never done before, we see ourselves as living among the stars. The boundaries of the known world are no longer primarily this planet or this galaxy. We are living in space; we now live in the galaxies. The worldview has dramatically shifted.

We now know that the universe is far more vast than we ever imagined possible. In very recent times, we have discovered inconceivable distances, the staggering immensity of the galaxies, suns and solar systems, black holes and dark stars. The boundlessness of our universe is only now *beginning* to dawn in human consciousness.

The four paradigm shifts we have looked at here have converged; these earthquake shifts have happened and are happening with incredible speed. Information, technology, economics, transportation advances, and communication systems of our time make us aware of these multiple paradigmatic shifts, which together create a megadigm of movement toward the future.

We live in a most extraordinary time. We are invited, therefore, to take even more seriously the content of preaching: the message of the Scriptures, the keys for living, the foundational life searches, and the major shifts of our time. The content of preaching draws on the wisdom of our day, the wisdom and experience of prior times, and the hopes and expectancies we have for the future. Preaching helps people in this new age.

Ways Forward

Pick one. You will discover the other three. That is my shorthand way of suggesting that you can grow the quality of your sermon content by selecting one of the four components of content we have discussed—Scripture, single aspects of living, foundational life searches, the major cultural shifts of our times.

You do not need to try to advance your understanding of all four. Pick one as the major focus you would have fun intentionally growing this year. The other three will come. Deepen your understanding of any one of these four, and you will discover that you will deepen your understanding of the other three. These components are dynamically interrelated.

For example, the individual aspects that advance living might be the component that currently interests you and that you would have fun exploring more fully. As you study this one in depth you will discover resources that advance your understanding of Scripture, the foundational life searches, and the major cultural shifts of our time as well.

You might decide that Scripture is your immediate "entry point" for developing the content of your sermons. Scripture will lead you to a deeper understanding of single aspects for living, the foundational life searches, and the major cultural shifts of our time.

Once you have selected one of the four to develop this year, decide how you would like to deepen your understanding of that area. I encourage you to consider some combination of one-time events, short-term study groups, a mentor-coach, and advanced seminars that will help you.

For example, let us say you have selected single aspects for living. Consider a one-time retreat you and others would have fun doing, with the focus being to deepen your understanding of the specific keys for a whole, healthy life that you plan to advance in your own life. Or you can decide to be part of a short-term study group of three to five sessions that explores together which of the keys to develop in each person's life.

You can invite a mentor-coach to share and work with you for a period of time as you explore these keys for living and which ones will be helpful to your own life. You can participate in an advanced seminar or continuing education event where the focus is on helping you grow the health and wholeness of your life.

Or you might decide that you have immediate interest in the major cultural shifts of our time. My suggestion is that you then select one of these earthquake shifts to study more deeply. For example, let's say you decide you want to understand more fully the dynamics of an excellent sprinter culture. Participate in a one-time retreat you and others would have fun doing. Let the focus be to deepen your understanding of the goals and values; the customs, habits, and traditions; the communications network; the leadership process; and the common shared vision of the future that are present in an excellent sprinter culture.

You can decide to be part of a short-term study group of three to five sessions that discovers together the dynamics of a sprinter culture. You can invite a mentor-coach to share and work with you for a period of time as you explore the ways in which a sprinter culture functions in people's lives. You can participate in an advanced seminar or continuing education event where the focus is on helping you deepen your understanding of a sprinter culture.

You will develop your sermon content as you grow your understanding of Scripture, the keys for living, foundational life searches, and the major cultural shifts of our time. Advance your understanding of one of these this year. Grow yourself with a combination of one-time retreat events, short-term study groups, a mentor-coach, and advanced seminars. The content of your preaching will deepen. Your people will grow in their understanding of the grace of God.

6

Motivation

Motivations stir. The motivations with which you prepare a sermon stir the motivations with which you preach. The motivations with which you preach stir the motivations with which your congregation listens to your sermon. The motivations with which your people listen stir the motivations with which they act on and live out the message you share.

Dave was new to the Christian movement. He found his way that morning to Michael's church. Dave's life had been solid and constructive. He had finished college, graduating with solid grades. He was working at a good job. He liked what he was doing. The plans for his marriage with Martha were moving forward. They had met in college, became good friends, and fell in love. They had been dating for three years, and the marriage was soon to be. Overall, he was doing well.

Yet he felt his life could be richer and fuller. His longing was for a deeper sense of meaning and purpose in his life. His yearning was for the closeness of community, of roots, place, and belonging. With the coming of his marriage to Martha, he was searching for a richer life of hope and compassion.

On that particular Sunday, he found his way to Michael's church. He had heard on the community grapevine that Michael's sermons were helpful for people.

That Sunday, as he did most Sundays, Michael shared his sermon with a sense of compassion and a spirit of community.

He shared it with the liveliness of good fun and good times. There was an energy and enthusiasm as he preached. Michael has fun in life, and he has fun in his preaching.

Michael's sermon, that Sunday, was helpful for Dave. The sermon was stirring and inspiring. It touched the hearts of many. The content of the sermon helped people advance their lives with confidence and assurance. People experienced the grace of God. Dave said later, "I hope I can have that much fun as a Christian. I hope I can share that much compassion with people." Dave remembers best the compassion and community with which the sermon was shared.

The Five Major Motivations

Motivation is internal, not external. Manipulation may be external, but motivation is clearly internal. Each day we draw on and experience many motivations. Some are healthy. Some are confusing. Some appeal to our lesser self. Some are hurtful and damaging to our development. In preaching, it helps to resonate with the healthy motivations that stir people to live life with grace and growth.

Five major motivations are helpful in preaching. More precisely, I refer to these as *motivational resources:*

1. Compassion
2. Community
3. Challenge
4. Reasonability
5. Commitment

These are the major motivational resources within each of us that we draw on to motivate ourselves to live whole, healthy lives. All five major motivations are present in each person. These five are the motivations that draw persons to the grace of God; help them become disciples; help them live whole, healthy lives; and help them give generously of their gifts, strengths, and competencies to the mission of God.

Within each person, one or two of these motivations tend to be predominant at a given point in that person's life pilgrimage. The same motivations may not be predominant at every point in a person's life. Life is pilgrimage. Life is search, growth, and development. Although all five are present, one or two are usually predominant. Were all five equally present, there would be too much diffusion. One or two dominant motivational resources help people have movement, action, and direction in their lives.

Likewise, in a sermon all five major motivations are present. In a helpful sermon, one or two will be predominant. In that fashion, the sermon will have a sense of movement and direction. When all five are equally emphasized, the sermon has a sense of diffusion and tends to go nowhere because it goes too many places at once. With one or two motivations dominant, the sermon has focus and direction. Let us look now at each of the five motivational resources.

1. *Compassion* is sharing, caring, giving, loving, and serving. Lots of people do what they do out of the motivation of compassion. Many helpful sermons share the motivational source of compassion.

2. *Community* is good fun, good times, roots, place, belonging, friends, and family. In our time, people have a profound search for community, not committees. In an earlier time, we heard, "Put So-and-so on a committee, and he will feel ownership in the church." In our time, when people discover a deep sense of community, they feel deep ownership in this congregation.

3. *Challenge* is attainment, accomplishment, and achievement. Many people rise to the bait of a challenge. For them, a rich source of motivation is a sense of attainment and accomplishment.

4. *Reasonability* is a major motivation. Reasonability has to do with data, analysis, logic, and "it makes good sense." I work with churches in Silicon Valley; they have a high density of engineers, scientists, and data processing experts. Reasonability is a major motivational resource there. I work with churches in small college towns where there is a high density of professorial types. There also, reasonability is a major motivational resource.

I worked with one church that had been "burned" seventeen years in a row. I don't mean the building had burned. They had tried something new each of the previous seventeen years and had gotten burned each time. That kind of experience will grow forward the major motivation of reasonability. "It had better make good sense before we go out on a limb with something else new. It had better be reasonable before we stick our hand into the flame again."

I honor this. Most people finally do not move forward solely because "it makes reasonable sense." I have never yet conducted a wedding for anyone, nor yet met a person who got married, who did so out of the motivation of reasonability. Most people get married out of a spirit of compassion and a sense of community and then, later, rationalize why it made good sense to get married when they did. Most people grow and develop, advance and build their lives out of a spirit of compassion and a sense of community.

5. *Commitment* is duty, vow, obligation, and loyalty. Some people do what they do out of a motivation of commitment. This is especially true of some persons who have been long-time Christians. Commitment is a motivational resource people develop later in their Christian pilgrimage.

To be sure, challenge, reasonability, and commitment are helpful. At the same time, for many people across their whole lives, the two predominant motivational resources out of which they live and move and have their being are a spirit of compassion and a sense of community.

Motivational Match and Gap

A *motivational match* occurs when the key leaders, grassroots persons, pastor, and staff in a congregation share the same motivational resources. For example, in many congregations the key leaders do what they do from a spirit of compassion and a sense of community. This resonates with the grass roots, who, in most congregations, primarily motivate themselves out of compassion and community.

The sermons the pastors deliver share a spirit of compassion and a sense of community. This resonates with the unchurched, who look for and long for congregations that deliver two things: a spirit of compassion and a sense of community.

In this scenario, all are on the same motivational wavelength (see Figure 6.1).

When you see congregations who consistently show a strong track record of action, implementation, and momentum, what you have discovered is a motivational match

Figure 6.1. A Motivational Match.

	Key Leaders	Grass Roots	Pastor and Staff	Unchurched
Compassion	•	•	•	•
Community	•	•	•	•
Challenge				
Reasonability				
Commitment				

between the preaching of the pastor and the motivational resources of the key leaders, grass roots, and unchurched. As a result of this motivational match, many people share in the mission, deliver the work, and give generously.

In contrast to this match, some congregations have a few people who are doing most of the work and giving most of the money. Whenever you find this situation, what you have found is evidence of a *motivational gap*.

A common motivational gap exists, for example, when the key leaders primarily motivate themselves out of challenge and commitment. These key leaders look for pastors who are like them. They look for pastors whose sermons focus primarily on challenge or commitment.

In meeting after meeting, the pastor and the key leaders reinforce each other on the motivations of challenge and commitment. They frequently lament, "If only people were more committed and could see the challenge, this dying venture would get better." Although they are on the same motivational wavelength, they miss the grass roots and will not reach the unchurched. As Figure 6.2 shows, there is no match.

The key leaders and pastor are transmitting on the radio frequencies of challenge and commitment, but the grass roots and the unchurched have their radios tuned to the stations of compassion and community. There is no resonance, no match.

Figure 6.2. A Motivational Gap.

	Key Leaders	Grass Roots	Pastor and Staff	Unchurched
Compassion		•		•
Community		•		•
Challenge	•		•	
Reasonability				
Commitment	•		•	

One of the mistakes some of us make is to assume that because we motivate ourselves in certain ways, we can help other people motivate themselves in the same ways. It is a serious mistake. It is helpful for us to be on the same motivational wavelength with the persons with whom we are developing rich, full relationships.

In giving and stewardship campaigns, you see the damage of a motivational gap: the grass roots respond less generously. When there is a motivational match of compassion and community, the grass roots give generously to the mission of the congregation.

When there is a motivational match, as shown in Figure 6.1, the preaching generates a strong track record of action, implementation, and momentum. When the preaching lives out a spirit of compassion and community, people discover keys for living whole, healthy lives. The congregation moves forward in God's mission. People grow and develop in the grace of God.

By contrast, when there is a motivational gap in preaching, as shown in Figure 6.2, the key grassroots persons do not respond. The leaders generally compliment the minister on "hitting the congregation a little harder this Sunday," but the sermon does not resonate with the grass roots, and it will not reach the unchurched. The result is that a few people do most of the work and give most of the money.

Compassion and Community

Preaching does not have to grow primarily out of commitment or challenge. Preaching is compassion. Discipleship is compassion. Stewardship is compassion. These statements are my shorthand way of affirming that, for the grass roots of the congregation and for unchurched persons in the community, the motivations of compassion and community are their primary motivational resources. For them, challenge, reasonability, and commitment are secondary motivational resources. Whenever the preaching stirs a spirit of compassion and a sense of community, the grass roots and the unchurched respond generously.

For the moment, right now, I want you to think of one of the happiest times in your life. It may be a time of a promotion. It may be a time of discovering new strengths, gifts, and competencies. It may be the time someone accepted your proposal of marriage. You ran down the hall saying, "We're getting married! We're getting married!" Perhaps it is the time when a child was born, and you ran down a hospital corridor saying, "It's a girl! It's a girl!" Perhaps it is a time of reunion of friends and family who for a long time have looked forward to being together.

Mostly, when we think of the happiest times in our lives, we think of events of compassion. The generosity of sharing and giving are richly present. Sometimes we are sharing our compassion. Other times we are the recipients of compassion. In the midst of these joyful times, we discover the grace of God in our lives.

When we think of these wonderful times, we think of gatherings of community, where we draw close together with one another. We picture the reunions where we hug and hold one another, laugh and eat, share remembrances and hopes. We think of good fun and good times, sharing and caring. We think of the wonder in discovering we are part of God's family. We experience the grace of God.

In thinking of our happiest times, our minds do not often picture times of challenge or reasonability or commitment. There may be some times that come to mind. For those of us who are high-challenge, deeply committed types, we can probably come up with a few. But even then, when we think of joyful times, we tend to talk of events of compassion and gatherings of community.

Many of the biblical images of Jesus are settings of community and stories of compassion. In the closing of the Gospel of John, near the end of Christ's time with his disciples, Jesus does not say, "Peter, will you make the commitment? Peter, will you rise to the challenge?" He could have asked these two questions. It is near the end. One might expect Jesus to focus on those motivations. It is significant that Christ does not do so.

What Jesus does say is, "Peter, do you love me?" Compassion. "Yes, Lord, you know that I love you." Then Jesus says, "Peter, feed my sheep." Community. Jesus invites his disciples to the motivations of compassion and community.

People care about what ministers know, when they know the minister cares. Again and again across the years, people say to me, "Dr. Callahan, please help us find a minister who will come and love us and whom we can come to love."

How many people do you know who are happily married who say to their spouse as they go to bed at night, "Now dear, remember your marriage vows." What people do who are happily married is share gestures of compassion and community. They hug and they kiss. Then they go to rest.

But the phrase, repeated and repeated in some congregations, is, "Now, remember your membership vows." "Remember your membership vows" sounds more like "Remember to clean up your room." How many people do you know who respond to this by leaping eagerly to clean up their room?

In the early years of the Christian movement, the membership vows were more like these:

Will you love the Lord your God with all your heart, and mind, and soul, and strength?

Will you love Christ as your Lord and Savior?

Will you love your neighbor as generously as you love yourself?

Will you live a life of grace and peace, compassion and community?

It took the Christian movement more than nineteen hundred years to produce institutional membership vows that sound like "Will you be loyal to such-and-such a denominational church and uphold it by your prayers, your presence, your gifts, and your support?" In the early days, there were no denominations in existence. The focus was on the movement more than on the institution.

I want you to know that I am not knocking commitment. Commitment made the list. It is the last one on the list, not because it is least important, nor because it is lesser than the other motivations. It is where it is on the list because it is a motivational resource that grows forward later in our Christian pilgrimage. The early motivations that draw us to Christ are compassion and community. Then, over a period of ten, fifteen, or twenty years, some people grow forward the motivation of commitment.

When somebody says to me, "Dr. Callahan, what we need in this church are people with more commitment," I say to them, "Good friend, you have just taught me that you are a long-time Christian. And if there were lots of long-time Christians out there, we could develop forward the movement on the basis of commitment. But what is out there are people who do not yet know Christ." Then I go on to help them remember what drew them to the Christian movement in their earliest years. They generally share their early experiences of finding love and home, compassion and community. The people we hope to reach are where they were. This is a beginning time.

Some books focus on stewardship as commitment. Some focus on discipleship as commitment. But whenever you see books like this, simply know that they were written by long-time Christians. In fact, we need more books whose focus is on stewardship as compassion, on discipleship as community. These books resonate with the grassroots persons and the unchurched.

In our time, we need more high-compassion congregations. Some congregations think of themselves as high-commitment congregations. When you look closely at these congregations, what you discover are persons on the staff team and volunteers in the congregation who are legendary for their shepherding, their sense of compassion, and their spirit of community. The primary reason high-commitment churches work is because of the presence of high compassion shared by the staff and the grass roots.

The text does not say, "For God was so challenged by the world . . ." God may very well be challenged by the mess we are making of this world, but what the text says is, "For God so loved the world . . ." The text says, "Love your neighbor." It doesn't say, "Be committed to your neighbor." The text says, "Look how they love one another," not "Look how they are reasonable with one another."

I Corinthians 13 is a remarkable passage affirming the grace of God. It does not close with the words, "Now abide challenge, reasonability, and commitment, and the greatest of these is commitment." The text, in fact, says, "Now abideth faith, hope, and compassion, and the greatest of these is compassion."

Yes, I do affirm that an aspect of preaching is commitment. Discipleship is commitment, stewardship is commitment—particularly for long-time Christians. But this is a beginning time. From the earliest beginning time, in the mission age of the first century, and now in the twenty-first century—a new age of mission—preaching is compassion. Preaching is community.

Motivations and Preaching

In helpful preaching, there is a resonance between the minister and the congregation in terms of the motivations that live themselves out in the sermon. As you think of this dynamic between motivations and preaching, be conscious of (1) the motivations with which you prepare a sermon and (2) the motivations with which you preach the sermon. Also be conscious of (3) the motivations present in the content of the sermon itself.

As you consider your congregation, give thought to (1) the motivations that your listeners bring with them, (2) the motivations they discover as you preach, and (3) the motivations with which they act on and live out the message you share.

For example, when we preach, our people may discover the motivation with which we prepare rather than the motivation present in the sermon. Sometimes the motivation present in us as we prepare is an internal motivation of challenge. For whatever reasons, perhaps because we are discouraged over something that has happened in the congregation or in our lives, as we work on the sermon, the motivation of challenge is present.

Thus the sermon is delivered with the motivation of challenge. The *subject* of the sermon might be compassion, but what people discover, by the manner in which the sermon is preached—namely with challenge—is a spirit of challenge rather than a message of compassion. In effect, the sermon *challenges* people to compassion. This may resonate with the key leaders of your congregation, but it will not resonate well with the grass roots.

When the motivation with which we prepare the sermon is a spirit of compassion, and the subject of the sermon is compassion, then there is a higher probability that the sermon will be shared with a spirit of compassion. The motivational match of preparation, spirit of delivery, and sermon subject will resonate richly with the congregation.

I was once leading a preaching seminar at Duke University. At the break, three pastors came up to me bubbling with excitement. They said to me, "Dr. Callahan, we now understand what our people have been trying to tell us."

Each of these pastors, in his own way, lived out a spirit of compassion and a sense of community Monday through Saturday in their ministry. They were good shepherds with their congregations and their communities. They loved their people, and their people loved them. Each was, in fact, the key pastor for the community in which each served.

On Sunday morning, however, they seemed weighted down by the institutional baggage of trying to keep the venture afloat. What kept showing up were sermons on challenge and commitment. Their people would leave saying, "Pastor, you don't seem quite like yourself this morning." These pastors *did not* seem like themselves, because they were not themselves. In the seminar discussions about motivations, these three pastors had found a new, fresh way forward.

You may discover that there is a motivational gap in your congregation. Your key leaders may be motivated primarily by commitment, challenge, or reasonability, or by some combination of these three. By contrast, you may find that compassion and community primarily motivate the grassroots people of your congregation.

One way forward might be to share, on eight out of twelve Sundays, sermons with a spirit of compassion and a sense of community. These sermons will be a motivational match with the grass roots and the unchurched. On the other four

Sundays, the sermons might build on the motivations of challenge, reasonability, or commitment. These sermons will resonate with your key leaders.

Were you to reverse this, with eight sermons of challenge, reasonability, or commitment, you will miss the grass roots and not reach the unchurched. Given the times in which we live, only four sermons over three months that build on compassion and community will not be sufficient for the age of mission and for the people God gives us to serve.

Certainly, I encourage you to develop an understanding with your key leaders. Help them understand the motivations that draw new persons to Christ, that help them become disciples, and that help them contribute generously of their strengths, gifts, competencies, and resources to the mission of God.

Know this: anxiety, fear, anger, and rage are demotivators, not motivators. We all have our fair share of anxiety in this life's pilgrimage. Sometimes, anxiety becomes fear. Fear then becomes anger, and, occasionally, anger turns into rage. Some sermons build on anxiety and fear. Some sermons are really displaced anger.

We can motivate people to do something out of anxiety and fear. However, they mostly respond in lesser ways. They respond in richer ways when we help them motivate themselves out of compassion, community, challenge, reasonability, or commitment. Under threat, people wither. With compassion and encouragement, people grow.

Commitment is a healthy, whole, constructive motivational resource. It is therefore inappropriate for a sermon to use "commitment" as the guise for a thinly veiled anger. It is a misuse of an honorable motivation to imply, in a sermon, that "If you people were only more committed, this church would be better." What is really happening in such a sermon is that the minister is in effect saying, "I am displacing my anger onto you because things are not moving as rapidly as I had hoped they would."

Commitment invites people to their deepest loyalties. It is a healthy motivational resource. Commitment is not displaced anger. Sermons built on anxiety or fear, anger or rage, may temporarily move people to something. But, mostly, they cause people to be tense, tight, nervous, and anxious. Then people do less well. They do better when they are encouraged with the constructive motivational resources of compassion, community, challenge, reasonability, or commitment.

Helpful preaching invites people to develop forward whole, healthy lives. Such sermons build on people's healthy motivational resources. In encouraging and inviting ways, these sermons help people to advance their lives in the light of the grace of God.

7

Delivery

How you deliver your sermon shapes how and what people hear and what they do in their lives as a result of the sermon. A person's perception of reality *is* reality to that person. Your delivery contributes to how people perceive your sermon and, therefore, how they receive it.

Across the years, I have had the privilege of hearing many sermons. I am grateful for the many ministers who have shared them. Their sermons have enriched my own life. Sunday after Sunday, with remarkable presence, pastors share the good news of grace. The content of their sermons is solid and helpful. They live and preach with a spirit of compassion and a sense of community. Most of these ministers have solid delivery; they have shared their sermons with confidence and assurance.

Confidence breeds confidence. If you deliver your sermon with confidence and assurance, people will receive your sermon in a spirit of confidence and assurance. Your delivery stirs their confidence and assurance that they can move forward. Your solid delivery helps them both to receive your sermon and to act on it in their own lives.

By contrast, a weak, timid delivery leads people to perceive it as weak and timid, and they will receive the sermon and the ideas it contains in a weak, timid way. It is doubtful that people in the congregation will do anything in their lives as a result of such a sermon. If they act in any way, they will tend to do so with a weak, timid response.

Likewise, a harsh, demanding delivery yields a harsh, demanding perception. Listeners will frequently receive such a sermon in a way that results in their reacting with passive-aggressive behavior, low-grade hostility, subliminal resentment, and eruptive forms of anger. Neither a weak, timid delivery nor a harsh, demanding delivery advances the sermon. Each gets in the way of people's hearing the message of grace in the sermon.

Recently, I was leading a seminar on preaching. We were having a remarkable time. People in the seminar were discovering their strengths for preaching and the possibilities they have for advancing their preaching. I had just finished the section on delivery.

During the break, one of the participants told me about his brother, who works in the movie industry. When we convened, I invited him to share with the whole group what he had just shared with me.

During the previous year, his brother had an appointment with Charlton Heston, at Heston's home. When he arrived, he was greeted warmly at the door. He was told that Mr. Heston was not there but would be shortly. He was invited in and treated courteously while he waited twenty or thirty minutes. When Heston came in, he was gracious and apologetic. He was running late for his appointment because he had been delayed at his weekly session with his speech coach. His *speech* coach.

The seminar participant sharing this experience concluded his story by saying, with considerable appreciation, "*God* has a speech coach; *Moses* has a speech coach." He was deeply impressed, as we all were, that one of the most competent speakers of our time works regularly on his delivery.

This story stirred my own thinking. I shared with the preaching seminar my own reflection that, across the years, many of the solid speakers I have had the privilege of know-ing are persons who work regularly on their delivery. I am deeply impressed with the vast number of ministers who seek to advance their sermon delivery.

The Dynamics of Delivery

We can draw on the remarkable resources available in our time. We can advance our eye contact, facial expressions, ges-tures, stance, and voice so that the message of the sermon is strengthened by solid delivery.

Eye Contact

We help our sermon with a strong start when, in the first few minutes of the sermon, we establish direct eye contact with our congregation. And for many people, the sermon begins when we step to the pulpit (or to whatever space whence the sermon is to be shared), regardless of whatever we might do before we begin the "official" sermon—for example, read the Scripture or have a brief one-sentence prayer. When minis-ters with solid delivery step to the pulpit, they intentionally use these first several minutes to establish direct, personal eye contact with their people.

In one congregation, the minister came forward, stood at the pulpit, established direct eye contact with his people, and began the sermon by saying, "I will lift up mine eyes unto the hills from whence cometh my help." As he spoke, he looked warmly at his people, established eye contact, and then lifted his eyes up. By contrast, in another congregation, I observed a minister preaching on the same text. He came to the pulpit and *read*, looking down, "I will lift up mine eyes unto the hills." He proceeded to read a manuscript.

I encourage you to be free enough from your manuscript or notes that you have solid eye contact throughout the sermon. Some of the earliest preaching, as best as we can discern, was built on the personal experience the disciples shared with Jesus. They discovered the grace of God through the life, death, and resurrection of Christ. The good news of grace filled their preaching. My sense is that the custom of manuscript preaching was a later addition. Sometimes I have the sense that a manuscript is more at home in a university than with a congregation.

When you find it helpful to prepare a sermon manuscript, I encourage you to do so. This method of preparing sermons is useful for many ministers. Some find that detailed notes are more helpful to them. Some find that an outline works well for them. Prepare a manuscript, detailed notes, or an outline—whatever helps you. What you use may vary from Sunday to Sunday. Developing manuscripts as part of preparation is frequently helpful.

We know this, though: people learn less well when we are reading a manuscript, looking up only now and then. When we are mostly reading, looking down, our listeners lose both eye contact and our facial expressions. These are significant losses. Further, people teach me that in these situations, they have the sense the minister does not know the material well enough to share personally and warmly with them.

In my early years, I found a manuscript helpful. Over time, I have learned not to be a slave to it. I encourage you, at a bare minimum, to know at least the first three minutes and the last three minutes so well that you establish excellent eye contact and helpful facial expressions during the beginning and ending of the sermon. People want to know what we think, believe, feel, and have confidence in, not what we read to them.

As I will be discussing further in Chapter Eight, people remember the first three minutes and the last three minutes of a sermon. The first three minutes are important; so too are the concluding moments. Eye contact during these two times is helpful to the delivery of the sermon. Start strong. Finish strong.

I have found it helpful to begin to establish eye contact with people even before the service actually starts. I look first for my family and close friends. Then I look for other healthy people in the congregation—mentors, leaders, and grassroots people. I look for the children and the youth of our congregation. I look for the elderly. I look for first-time worshipers and long-time workers. I seek to begin strong and grow stronger in my eye contact with the congregation.

Then I can establish eye contact with the one or two people who are the "loyal opposition" of every pastor. Then I develop eye contact with the persons who have almost learned how to "push my buttons" and who try to create a codependent–dependent relationship with me. I have learned that when I establish eye contact with them first, they have stirred my desire to be too helpful, and I then have a tendency to deliver too much help in the sermon.

The art of a sermon is to deliver almost enough help to be helpful, but not so much help that the help becomes harmful and creates a codependent–dependent pattern of preaching. In the parable of the Samaritan, the innkeeper delivers just enough help that the man, beaten and robbed, can be on his journey. There is nothing in the parable to suggest that the innkeeper delivered so much help that the man, in appreciation and codependency, lived, lo, the rest of his days with the innkeeper. God delivers to us just enough help that we can be on our journey. A helpful sermon does the same.

When I begin the sermon, I usually repeat the same sequence of establishing eye contact with which I began the worship service. I vary the pattern from time to time. I have found it helpful to begin where I am most at home and move from there to the people who are new; then to those who are sometimes difficult to deal with and to those who seek a code-pendent relationship.

Eye contact is decisive in getting a sermon across. Your eye contact teaches people you are a good shepherd. It teaches people you have confidence and assurance in what you are sharing. It teaches people that the message is part of you, that you have internalized it well. It teaches people you love them as their pastor.

Facial Expressions and Lighting

In solid delivery, the facial expressions of the minister match the message of the sermon. When the focus of the sermon is compassion, it is helpful to have facial expressions that share love and compassion. The message and the messenger share the same message. Occasionally, I have allowed myself to become caught up in challenging people to compassion. The message and the messenger became incongruous. The message was compassion, but the facial expressions communicated challenge. Dissonance was the result. When my facial expressions are open and inviting, warm and compassionate, they match the message of compassion in the sermon.

Some years ago, on a Christmas Sunday, I watched one pastor preach a sermon on the subject of joy. Yet something must have distracted him from his message. Doom and gloom suffused his face as he muddled his way through that sermon. His facial expressions, with their shadows of despair and discouragement, were not kind to him or to his sermon.

When I begin a sermon, I find it helpful to smile. I live with the confidence that a sermon is a great banquet of God's grace, a wedding feast of God's hope. A sermon is a time of joy and wonder, new life and hope. It helps to smile. Now, I do not mean a slaphappy, nonsensical, silly type of smile filled with giddiness and glee. I hardly ever see that in ministers. Mostly, ministers have a sense of joy as they preach.

Occasionally I see a minister begin his sermon as though we were gathered at a funeral. Indeed, there are funerals that have more of a sense of joy and celebration than have some sermons. Frowns of doom and gloom do not advance good news.

Indeed, when you are sharing a tough point in your sermon, let your facial expression be relaxed and inviting. When our facial expressions are tense and tight, nervous and anxious, we create people who are tense and tight, nervous and anxious. They are less likely to be able to receive our point. People are more open and receptive when they are relaxed and having fun, and their spirit is at peace.

Years ago, I was given a picture of Christ smiling. It is a wonderful picture. It helps me know we are the Christmas people—the people of wonder and joy. We are the Easter people—the people of new life and hope. Yes, we are the people of the cross, and we can have a sense of joy that God so loved the world, and us, that God sent Jesus to be Christ with us. We are the people of Pentecost—the people of grace, compassion, community, and hope. God smiles. Amidst the difficulties and tragedies that abound, God continues to bless us with grace, compassion, and hope. We can be joyful for God's grace.

Lighting can complement or detract from one's facial expressions. Sometimes a minister's face is warm and inviting, but the lighting causes the face to be dark and shadowy. I speak in places where the builder or architect had installed a small white spotlight shining directly down over the pulpit. White light shining directly down creates distinct, harsh shadows underneath and on the sides of a person's face. The poor lighting and the resulting shadows create an illusion reminiscent of a caricature rather than a kindly visage. The facial expression is dark and gloomy.

Many congregations have been wise enough to install lighting that comes down from both sides at about a forty-five-degree angle, using a combination of white light, soft-colored flood lights, and spotlights. They know that a soft rose light creates warmth, a soft yellow washes away shadows, and a soft blue adds depth. The best lighting for a speaker's face comes in at an angle rather than directly from above.

In some churches, the pulpit is on the side. In other churches, there is a center pulpit. When a minister discovers the possibility of moving about during the sermon—that the pulpit need not be an anchor that weighs one down in one spot—this opens a new avenue of communication with the congregation. In these circumstances, it is wise for the minister to learn both the strengths and the boundaries of the lighting.

Frequently, simple adjustments can be made in the lighting so that, as the minister moves about, there continues to be adequate light directly on the minister's face. In this way, the congregation can clearly see the minister's facial expressions. The sermon takes on a personal warmth. What is undesirable and distracting is for the minister to move from well-lighted areas into semilit or deep, shadowy, unlit areas.

Frequently, I encourage designers to include adequate lighting at the area of the altar rail. During the planning for building one of the finest churches in this country, I told the architect, "We have a minister who likes to walk down into the open area at the altar rail at the end of the service to welcome people. When people join the church, he stands with them there. We want to be sure to plan lighting for this area." It took thoughtful planning and several adjustments to achieve generous lighting so as to avoid having the minister walk from light into shadows. Even with the prior planning, it took several adjustments to achieve adequate lighting. Until the lighting was adjusted, the congregation lost the ability to see the minister's face when he moved away from the pulpit area.

One principle I have is, "The larger the space, the warmer the face." Sometimes a congregation moves into a larger sanctuary, and the response is that the space feels remote and unfriendly. Two things help. First, we achieve very adequate lighting of the faces of the persons leading the service and sharing the sermon. Second, we encourage the worship leaders and the pastor to focus on facial expressions that communicate a spirit of compassion and a sense of community, a spirit of warmth and a sense of confidence and assurance.

As you deliver your sermon, feel free to share warm, gracious, lively facial expressions. Further, I encourage you to make any necessary adjustments to the lighting in the areas where you are. With the warmth of your spirit and the liveliness and compassion of your facial expressions, your sermons will be more personal and helpful.

Gestures and Stance

Both gestures and stance strengthen one's delivery. Calvin Heinz was my speech teacher and debate coach in high school. He was tall, with graying hair and a stately manner. His spirit was warm, generous, and relaxed. He was instrumental, in my early years, in helping me understand the value of gestures and stance for enriching and enhancing the message.

I can see him now, sitting in the back row, relaxed, with his right arm draped across the top of the row. It was his way of encouraging us to relax, to have an inviting spirit, and to share gestures that were open and inviting, to have a stance that was confident and assured. Since those days of his generous help with me, I have encouraged many to develop gestures and stance that are inviting and encouraging, that put people at ease.

Open hands help. A closed fist, with the index finger pointing, does not necessarily connote positive thoughts. When we want to get across a point that will advance and encourage our people, a pointing finger looks, regrettably, more like scolding. By contrast, our gesture can be invitational: an open hand, extended to the congregation in an inviting way.

Sometimes the best thing to do with our hands is to let them be at our sides in a relaxed, natural, confident way. Busy hands are distracting. One minister shared with me that, in his excitement for his sermon, he would move his hands and arms in quick, disjointed, hurried movements, virtually without realizing that he was doing so. One of his senior members, wise and caring, took him aside one day and helped him discover a more relaxed, generous way of letting gestures support rather than distract from the message.

We do not always need to be doing something with our hands. Often, it is helpful simply to let our hands flow naturally with the message we are sharing. We can be aware that folded hands sometimes create the appearance of a "closed spirit." Hands in one's pockets suggest, to some people, the impression of an "indifferent spirit," not a relaxed one.

Sometimes it helps to practice gestures as we practice the sermon. It is equally helpful to "practice" a relaxed, inviting spirit. Then our gestures flow naturally. They become part of who we are and the message we are sharing. Preaching is invitational. Our gestures can be invitational.

Likewise, how we stand and how we move are part of our delivery. When we stand in a relaxed, natural way, we come across as warm, open, and inviting. The spirit we communicate is one of grace. By contrast, a slouching posture does not come across as casual; it comes across as indifferent. Being rigid in one's stance communicates a stern, tense spirit. The feeling is one of law more than grace.

I have learned to stand with one foot slightly ahead of the other rather than to have both feet side by side. As in sports, when one foot is slightly ahead of the other, it is easier to move in any direction. When we place our two feet side by side, it takes more effort to move. The result is that some people seem to just "plant" and stay in that one spot.

Some movement helps, yet at the same time it is possible to move too much. A certain amount of movement is worth doing. Too much movement is distracting. Depending on the shape of the sanctuary and how the chairs and pews are arranged, I sometimes move several feet to one side as I am making a point. Then I may move several feet to the other side. I don't stride back and forth across the full width of the area.

Some sanctuaries are open and generous in design. They encourage thoughtful movement. In some worship centers, however, if we move too much to one side, some people have to twist their necks significantly to see us. In a sanctuary built "in the round," it is hard to figure out where "behind you" is. We can choose two-thirds of the round to be our primary focus of eye contact, and occasionally include the remaining third. Pick whatever two-thirds feels natural to you. Sometimes you can let the choir—when it is part of the round—be the one-third.

In many sanctuaries built in our time, there is no pulpit. Often, when there is a pulpit, it looks more like a music stand. In family worship centers, there is an effort to have us share worship as family together without anything separating leaders and congregation. In an earlier time, the minister stood behind a pulpit to communicate that "this, now, is the word of God." Many ministers are moving beyond this formal, institutional sign of validation, seeking a congregational focus on family worship. The effort is to be a congregation more than a cathedral.

I used to cling to the pulpit as a source of security. It was more than a place to put my manuscript. By holding onto its substantial form, I hoped it would help me deal with my anxiety level as I preached. Over time, I discovered that I needed to deal with my anxiety level in my head and heart, not by focusing on where I stood. I remember leaving the security of the pulpit one Sunday and discovering that my anxiety level was about the same as when I was behind it.

As students, we all watched many of our professors teach from their lectern in seminary classrooms. Some professors who stood at the lectern were helpful, yet the professors I remember most from my seminary days are those who were freed from the lectern and could share with us spontaneously and personally. These professors are my mentors.

Your worship center may have a pulpit, and your best wisdom may be to use it. Frequently, when I preach, that is my choice. It is not so much where we stand as how we stand. Our gestures and our stance can communicate a relaxed, confident, generous spirit of grace and hope.

Voice, Tone, and Inflection

Our voice, tone, and inflection contribute to the message of the sermon. The speed, rhythm, and pace of our voice advance the message. In our sermons, we are inviting people to a life of confidence and assurance. We do not speak, therefore, with a weak, timid, almost hesitant voice and inflection. We confidently invite people to the grace of God. The tone and inflection of our voice share invitation and confidence.

Your voice, tone, and inflection are ways you can share yourself, personally and constructively. With your voice, people discover the emotions present in you as you share the sermon. Rather than detracting from or diminishing your sermon, the tone and inflection of your voice can share your emotions, confidence, and assurance as you preach.

For some ministers, showing emotion is not a problem. For some of us, the problem is that we tend to hide our feelings. But we can share our emotions without "overdoing it." We can share our passion. The tone and inflection of our voices can communicate that we care wholly and fully about what we are sharing in this sermon. To be sure, some of us are more emotional than others. Quiet, confident passion is richer, fuller, and more convincing than loud, noisy passion. A sermon with some passion is more convincing that one without passion.

The pace of the sermon may include both a swiftly moving progression of ideas and the sharing of more leisurely described illustrations. The points can be shared sequentially, one after another, or they can be shared now here, now there, interspersed with narratives, stories, analogies, and examples. As we have already discussed, in our time it is helpful for the pace of many sermons to feel like the pace of an excellent sprinter. The sermon has good movement. It is highly intensive. It moves forward. Occasionally, it may have the pace of a solid marathon runner—it may be a slow, steady, building-to-a-final-point sermon.

Look at the possibilities for delivery we have discussed here: (1) eye contact, (2) facial expressions and lighting, (3) gestures and stance, and (4) voice, tone, and inflection. Identify your current strengths. Which of these do you have fun with and do well? Claim them. Then pick one of your current strengths that you would have fun growing. Build on your strengths. Do better what you do best. Then select one that perhaps is a midrange competency, and add it as a new strength.

Developing Your Delivery

Ministers grow their delivery with practice. You can advance your delivery skills in four helpful areas: with community groups, a speech coach, a speech group, and with a coaching team.

Community Groups

One of the best ways you can grow your delivery skills is as you speak in community groups. Find opportunities for speaking to a rich range of community groups. Mostly, you will share an inspirational, helpful speech. On occasion, you may share an "after-dinner speech," but more often than not you will benefit the community group with helpful, insightful contributions to the members' lives.

Focus your speech on an area of life with which you would have fun helping people. Identify a human hurt and hope, a life stage, or a community concern. Search your own life. Visit with people in the community groups you look forward to speaking to. Discover an interest that appeals to you and will be helpful to the groups with whom you look forward to being.

With wisdom and wit, craft a twenty-plus-minute sermon. At the end of your speech, people will have handles of help and hope, specific things they can do that will help them grow forward their lives. You only need one speech that is well done, delivered with wisdom and wit.

People in your congregation belong to a variety of groups: professional, vocational, helping, nonprofit, civic and community, hobby and interest, and recreational. Select the groups you would have fun speaking to, and discover a way to be invited to speak to five. Enlist the help of persons in your congregation. Do the speech well in three of the five. Be open to the ten invitations that will come. Be helpful in seven of these ten. Be open to the next ten invitations that will now come more quickly. Be helpful in seven of these ten.

Over the course of one or two years, seek out and speak to approximately twenty-five groups, and you will find that you have markedly improved your delivery. In community groups, the *only* thing you have going for you is the wisdom and wit of your message and your delivery. There is no thirty-minute warm-up of music, Scripture reading, responsive reading, and hymns. There is no choir, no stained-glass windows. There is no loyal group who comes year after year and who "belong" to this church.

You will strengthen your delivery speaking to these community groups. The bonus is that you need to invest only about fifty hours across the one or two years (including travel time) as you use these opportunities to improve your delivery. Further, the happy by-product is that you will have helped, depending on the size of the groups, four hundred to seven hundred persons with their lives. How long would it take you to do that going house by house? You will become a legend as a helpful, shepherding pastor.

Many ministers advance their delivery this way. As Paul is preaching to the people of Athens, he is developing his delivery. As Wesley is preaching to groups of miners outside the entrances to their mines, he is growing his delivery. In community groups, we have two things going for us: (1) the wisdom and the wit of our message and (2) the way we deliver that message.

Speech Coach
Another way you can advance your delivery skills is with a speech coach. Remarkably, that's what Charlton Heston does each week.

Search out the legendary speech coach in your area. There is likely to be one, perhaps at a nearby high school. The National Forensic Society has some excellent speech teachers. Sometimes you will discover a speech coach who is helping some of the leading business and community people, who are pros in their own speaking. You can contact a nearby college or university. You can be in conversation with the National Speakers Bureau. You can visit with several excellent speakers and invite them to share with you the name or names of their own speech coaches.

Look for a coach who can directly help you. Decide which of the aspects of delivery you plan to advance: eye contact, facial expressions, gestures and stance, or voice. Obviously, you look forward to receiving help with all these areas, and excellent coaches will resource you in all of them. At the same time, let your coach know the specific aspects with which you want help.

Select a speech coach with whom you do not plan to be good friends at the end of your coaching sessions. We select a golf pro who will help us with our irons or woods, not one who will be our good friend. We select a quilting instructor based on the person's ability to help us advance a specific area of quilting, not on whether they will be good friends with us. The same is true of piano teachers, singing coaches, woodworking teachers, and so on. Although friendship is a possibility, what we really want is the help of these experts' coaching and expertise so that we can develop our competencies in that specific area.

You are not looking for the well-meaning speech coach who would be glad to help you. That person may be willing, but you are searching for the coach who will do this job *well*. Therefore, you want to look for the speech coach who hardly has the time for you because he or she is working with so many excellent speakers in the area. You will have found the pro.

You can contract with your speech coach to work with you for a five-week period, in short-term, highly intensive sessions. After that period, take some time to practice more fully what you have learned. Then your speech coach can work with you for another five-week period. You will notice that I am inviting you to think like an excellent sprinter as you plan to use the resources of a speech coach.

Your speech coach can work with you for an hour and a

half on Saturday before you preach on Sunday. In this way, the focus will be directly on the immediate sermon you are preaching. Alternatively, your coach can help you as together you review a video of the sermon you preached the Sunday before. Or your coach can work with you for five sessions on whatever you want help with, which may not have any direct connection to the sermon for the coming Sunday. You don't have to set your coaching sessions around a specific sermon. The goal is to advance your delivery.

Speech Group

Another way to improve your delivery is to participate in a speech group that meets weekly or monthly. Participate in the group for a specific period of time, perhaps one year. In major metropolitan areas you may find the National Speakers Association. In many metropolitan areas and county seat towns, you will find a Toastmasters group.

Toastmasters groups include some of the leading civic, business, and community persons in the area. They are not there as amateurs. When you find yourself in a Toastmasters group, you are usually with a group of pros whose speaking is already solid, and they want to grow it toward excellence. One of the side benefits of participating in such a group is that you and these leaders will mutually benefit from meeting each other. Through the speeches they share you will learn much about them and their work. Further, you will learn much about the community you serve.

You may decide that a group of pastors and community leaders can share in the fun of a retreat together. You do not go off on a retreat to reinforce patterns of behavior that are not helpful. Instead, bring someone from Toastmasters—or a very gifted speech coach—to resource all of the participants. In the process, you also resource each other.

Coaching Team

Another way forward is to select two or three persons to work with you several times during the year as your "delivery" coaching team.

On one of your major Sundays, have your coaching team there to hear you. Alternatively, you can videotape your sermon. Then in the middle of that next week, gather with your coaching team. When I am on a coaching team, we frequently work with a tape. Together we look at the video, stopping it now here, now there, and we discover ways forward and suggestions that will advance and improve delivery.

With your coaching team, take the lead and share your best wisdom as to how you assess your delivery of the sermon. Assess the strengths and weaknesses of the delivery and share your thoughts as to specific possibilities for improvement. Then invite your coaching team to share their feedback and wisdom and their specific suggestions for how you can advance and develop your delivery.

This is not something you gather to do the Sunday afternoon after preaching that morning. Do not do it on Monday. Make it Tuesday, Wednesday, or Thursday. Most important, do not gather with your coaching team over Sunday lunch. Both you and they need time—a chance to reflect on what would be helpful—so that you can productively share together when you meet.

You can decide to have a coaching team help you over a three-month period. Or you can focus on four major Sundays. Pick the Sundays in the year that you know your sermon will be among your richest and fullest. Do not pick Sundays when you are likely to be off your game. Do not go overboard and have a coaching team work with you each week for a full year; you do not need that much help. You can invite them to help you two or three times during the year.

Ways Forward

As you can see, the art of advancing your delivery involves two steps. First, select the specific aspect of delivery you want to develop: eye contact, facial expressions, gestures and stance, or voice. You can choose any of these possibilities. I encourage you to select the specific area you would have fun advancing this year. Looking long-term, you can select three to work on overall: do one this year, one next year, one the year following. It is not needful that you focus on all areas of delivery at one time. Pick one area that you sense will help you advance your delivery and that you will have fun growing.

Second, select the way you plan to advance that area. You can choose speaking to community groups, working with a speech coach, sharing in a speech group, or working with a coaching team. In a given year, you may decide to benefit from one now and, in another year, you may choose to benefit from one of the others. Choose the one you will have fun doing.

I say "fun" because I encourage you to look for coaching, not correcting. Sometimes we settle into a safe, bland delivery pattern because we do not want to experience any more of the correcting that we experienced in the past. We have had enough correcting to last four lifetimes. Coaching breeds coaching. A coaching approach to your delivery creates sermons that are coaching, not correcting. The way you grow forward your preaching is the way you will share your preaching.

When you are having fun growing your delivery, your sermons will take on the spirit of a wedding feast and a great banquet. When you choose ways to grow your delivery that are a chore, your sermons will be delivered as a chore. To paraphrase Paul, God loves a cheerful preacher. Do not preach out of duty or obligation. One of the foundations for preaching is that a sermon is a sacrament. When a sermon is a sacrament, delivery counts. Something as sacramental as a sermon invites excellent delivery.

8

Structure

How you structure your sermon shapes how and what people hear. The art of preaching is to structure your sermon so that people are drawn into the sermon from the beginning; discover clues to advance their lives in whole, healthy steps; and leave with the spirit to act on the message of the sermon.

By *structure* I refer more to the flow of the sermon than to the outline of the points being made. These points can be stated in a deductive fashion, much as is done in a carefully constructed lecture or debate speech. Or these points can be shared in an inductive spirit, by which people discover the key points of the sermon almost as though they come upon them without realizing they are there. However the minister covers the points, people again and again teach me that they do not remember sermon outlines. Indeed, ministers frequently do not remember their own sermon outlines within days of having preached a given sermon.

What key leaders and grassroots people in congregations teach me is that they remember four things:

1. The first three minutes
2. The last three minutes
3. The strengths of the sermon
4. The warm moments of the sermon

These are the four components that stick with people, the four dynamics that advance the structure and flow of your sermon.

The First Three Minutes

Start strong. Grow stronger. The first three minutes of the sermon are decisive. As the adage goes, you never have a second chance to make a first impression. I encourage you to be conscious of the first impression of your sermon.

Your sermon begins when *you* begin. In a typical service of worship, just before the sermon, the congregation shares together in singing a stirring, inspiring hymn. Or the choir may share a remarkable anthem that leads people closer to the grace of God. It is consequential that what happens immediately before the sermon be stirring and inspiring, be helpful and hopeful, and lead people closer to the grace of God. Whatever happens immediately before the sermon sets the stage for the sermon.

If whatever happens immediately before a sermon is dull and deadly, boring and routine—the same innocuous thing Sunday after Sunday—then the sermon begins as if we have started out in a hole. If what happens immediately before the sermon is fresh and new, creative and inspiring, then the sermon has the chance to begin on high ground.

It is as we rise and walk to the pulpit that our sermon begins. Please do not think that a sermon starts *after* a sequence of events such as these: the minister walks to the pulpit or the center of the chancel, adjusts a coat or robe, looks down at the text with no eye contact with the congregation, reads the Scripture for the sermon, has some preliminary word of explanation about the Scripture, and then shares a hurried, routine prayer: "Let the words of my mouth and the meditations of my heart be acceptable in your sight, oh God."

The first three minutes start when we stand and walk to the pulpit or the center of the chancel and take our place to lead the congregation. People do not understand how the reading of the Scripture and the speaking of that routine prayer—all done mostly without making eye contact with them—do not count as part of the first three minutes of the sermon time.

You begin to shape the first impression of this sermon with whatever you do immediately following the congregational hymn or the anthem or whatever liturgical act happens immediately prior to your beginning. Know this: you begin when *you* begin. Thus, when you begin, *begin*. Take seriously the first three minutes. If only one thing can go well in this sermon, let the first three minutes go well.

That does not mean you invest your sermon preparation time in trying to discover what you are going to say and do in the first three minutes. Launch your preparation of the sermon. Begin praying, thinking, feeling, and writing the sermon. It may very well be that, toward the end of your preparation of the sermon, you will discover what to include in the first three minutes. You do not have to decide on the material for the first three minutes at the beginning of your preparation. You may find it as you are concluding your sermon preparation.

As I discussed in Chapter Seven, begin with solid eye contact with your congregation during the first three minutes. Gather the congregation with your eye contact, your sense of presence, and your sense of confidence and assurance. Let the first three minutes be the best part in the sermon. We do not get a second chance to make a first impression.

Share the central theme of your message within the first three minutes. You need not share the key points of the sermon in their full richness. People will discover these as the sermon unfolds. In the beginning, share your basic direction, simply, invitingly, in a suggestive, preliminary way. In the first three minutes, give your people the sense of where you are headed.

For the people of your congregation, the first three minutes of your sermon is the time when

Their creativity level is high

Their energy level is high

Their levels of anticipation and receptivity are high

Their anxiety level is low

Your people are in the best position to discover the direction of your sermon.

When you save the key point of your sermon until the very end, they will be hearing the central direction of the sermon at a time when

Their level of creativity is low

Their energy level is low

Their levels of anticipation and receptivity are, at best, low or now entirely absent

Their anxiety level has risen

People make better decisions about their lives and destinies when their creativity, energy, anticipation, and receptivity levels are high and their anxiety level is low. People tend to make no decision—or poor decisions—when their creativity, energy, anticipation, and receptivity levels are low and their anxiety level is high. When a sermon is dull and boring, anxiety levels rise because people feel their time has not been well spent, and they want the sermon to be over. When the sermon is stirring and inspiring, but the minister takes a long time to get to the key point, people's anxiety levels rise. They want some sense of healthy closure.

As we discussed earlier, there is the principle that in life 20 percent of the things we do deliver 80 percent of the "results." Eighty percent of the things we do deliver 20 percent of the results. The art of life is to focus on the 20 percenters that deliver 80 percent of the results, accomplishments, and achievements that make life worthwhile and satisfying.

Likewise, the art of preaching is to focus on the 20 percenters of life and to share the key 20 percenters of this sermon in the first three minutes. Help people know where you are headed early on. Share the key 20 percenters that shape 80 percent of the outcome of that sermon during the first three minutes.

It also is helpful for you to look over your sermon to be sure it contains no 80 percenters at all, or only a few. Some sermons chase rabbits. That is, they chase the 80 percenters that only deliver 20 percent of the results. Too much time can be wasted spent on the minor and incidental.

It is particularly important not to invest the first three minutes in minor, incidental material. Either you get people on board during the first three minutes, or they will not be with you during the remainder of that sermon. Your sermon will have left the dock, and the passengers are not on board the ship. There is no way they will come on board later in the sermon. You will have moved too far on your course. You can help people come on board with the sense of the direction this sermon is headed by letting them know at the beginning how it will be important, helpful, and decisive in their lives.

For example, the focus of your sermon might be on compassion. You can begin with an example. You might share a personal happening from your own life, wisdom, and experience. The illustration with which you begin helps people discover the focus of the sermon. Further, the beginning parable or story helps people become immediately involved in the sermon.

It is not so much that you begin your sermon by saying, "This morning I am going to talk about compassion." It is not so much that you share the whole of your sermon outline at the outset. It is interesting that the old expression "First tell them what you are going to tell them, then tell them, and tell them what you have told them" still persists. Sometimes this old adage may apply to a given sermon, particularly one in which you are breaking new, complex ground with your people. Usually, though, I encourage you to help your people come on board at the outset with an engaging, inviting beginning. Sometimes we are tempted to "save the best for last." The catch is that if our people are not with us in the beginning, they will not be there at the end to hear the "best" we saved. Start strong.

The Last Three Minutes

Finish well. Then quit. If a second thing can go well in your sermon, let it be the last three minutes. We never have a second chance to make a last impression, either.

I learned this the hard way. Early in my preaching, I counted more heavily than I do now on my manuscript to know what was next in the sermon. One Sunday I was sharing a sermon on a particular text. I was moving along well in the sermon. The congregation was with me. As I recall, the manuscript had about ten pages to it. Most of my manuscripts in those days did.

I would slide the next page of the manuscript to the left as I finished with it. I was on page eight, headed to a solid conclusion. The sermon was building to the finish I had planned. As I moved page eight to the left, I saw the dark wood of the pulpit before me. There was no page nine or ten. As I discovered later, I had somehow left the concluding two pages in my study. At that point in the sermon, my mind drew a blank.

There was a long pause. Followed by another, longer pause. I shuffled the manuscript to see if the concluding two pages had somehow been mixed in with the earlier pages. No luck. I finished as best I could, stumbling awkwardly, hesitantly to an end. It was painful. The congregation was kind enough to stay with me. The people continued to give me their attention, politely and decently enough, but what had been a solid sermon dwindled to a weak, feeble finish.

I learned a helpful lesson that day: know the last three minutes of the sermon as well as, if not better than, any other part. Finish strong.

The first three minutes of the sermon help people discover the wisdom and experience, compassion and hope of this sermon. The last three minutes of the sermon help people make decisions about their lives and look forward to the next sermon. In publishing circles, there is a saying that the first line of a book sells this book; the last line of a book sells the next book. My paraphrase of this theme is that the first three minutes sell this sermon; the last three minutes sell the next sermon. I further paraphrase the theme this way: the first three minutes sell this sermon; the last three minutes sell the next step people take to advance their lives.

Quit before people are ready for you to quit. They will look forward to your next sermon. Quit once. Do not have two, three, or four closings. Sometimes we are tempted to conclude with two or three closing illustrations. Use one. Sometimes we repeat our key theme two or three times in the closing. Say it once. Share with your people one sermon, not three sermons in one. Save something for the Sundays to come. Do just enough in this sermon that people can move forward in their life's journey.

The art of the sermon is to share with people just enough help to be helpful, but not more help than would be helpful. Otherwise the help becomes harmful. We do not want to create a pattern of codependency. The best ending is the one that ties together the ends of the sermon—with encouragement and hope—and ends.

Quit while you are ahead. You have convinced people of a helpful course of action for their lives. You have helped them discover—in fresh, new ways—the grace of God in their lives. Quit. When you go on to try to convince them yet a second or third time, you are raising doubts. You are creating second thoughts. You are overselling. You are unraveling what you have accomplished.

I was once visiting with a real estate broker. He is known throughout the community for his wisdom, integrity, and honesty. We were discussing the dynamics of selling a house. He said to me, "My biggest problem with some of my salespeople is that they oversell a house. A young couple will discover a house. They will examine it, fall in love with it, and be ready to buy it. But the salesperson keeps selling the house and, in the process of doing so, talks them out of the sale. My best salespeople know when the house is sold. They quit selling it right then."

Close well. Go for closure. Go for a sense of direction, decision, and future in people's lives and destinies. It is not so much that you issue to people a solemn command or a stern challenge. It is more that you share with people a joyful invitation to a new life in the grace of God. When you come to the end of the sermon, close your mouth, stop talking, and breathe a silent prayer of gratitude for God's grace in helping you to share this good news with your people.

Start well. Grow stronger. End well. Amen.

The Strengths of the Sermon

If a third thing can go well, let the strengths of the sermon be richly and fully present. The strengths of the sermon have to do with the integrity and value of the sermon. They have to do with the specific ways the sermon is helping people directly with their lives. The strengths of a sermon enhance the spirit of mutual trust and respect within the congregation that the sermon evokes and the spirit of confidence and assurance with which people grow forward in their lives.

The following are some of the specific strengths of a sermon:

- The sermon shares some insight helpful in daily life.
- The sermon stirs a longing to serve God's mission.
- The sermon helps us grow whole, healthy lives in the grace of God.
- The sermon is encouraging.
- The sermon helps us discover a spirit of compassion.
- The sermon helps us find a sense of community.

Helpful Insight

In a sermon that shares some insight helpful in daily life, the focus of the sermon is with the people of the congregation, not primarily with the pastor. Regrettably, I occasionally hear a sermon where the focus is primarily the pastor. The minister—beleaguered, battered, bruised, and worn out—sees the sermon as primarily meant for him. In effect, the minister is preaching to his own needs in comforting ways. In helpful preaching, the minister—with his own searches, difficulties, discoveries, and hopes—is certainly "included" in the sermon. But the sermon is not primarily for the minister. The sermon advances people's living of everyday, ordinary life.

Longing to Serve

When a sermon stirs a longing to serve God's mission, people hearing the sermon discover and rediscover the longings to serve that God has planted in their hearts. People want their lives to count. God gives them longings to serve in mission. We are put here for a purpose. People want to live a theology of service, not a theology of survival.

Regrettably, I sometimes hear a sermon that is what I call a one-cell, closed sermon. The congregation—for a variety of reasons, but frequently because the people have been scared and scarred—has developed a one-cell, closed church. The people have "huddled up" in a defensive, self-protective way. Groups who are insecure about their own relationships tend to be closed groups. Usually, when you find a cliquish, exclusive group, you have found an insecure group. The one-cell, closed sermon contributes to that sense of being closed, clannish, cliquish, and exclusive.

In helpful preaching, the sermon nurtures the congregation to be warm, welcoming, inviting, open, and inclusive. Open groups are secure in their relationship with one another. It is precisely their confidence in their relationships, with one another and with God, that enables them to be open and inclusive of new persons. A helpful sermon nurtures the best instincts in a congregation to be open, inclusive, warm, and welcoming. Sadly, a one-cell, closed sermon nurtures the lesser, weaker tendencies in a one-cell church.

Sometimes I hear a two-cell sermon. Some congregations are two-cell churches. The best thing two-cell churches do is fight. There are the old-timers, and there are the newcomers. Now, the newcomers aren't that new. They may have come thirty years ago, but, from the vantage point of the old-timers, they are new. The fight is on.

Sometimes a sermon takes sides with the old-timers. Sometimes it takes sides with the newcomers. In some cases, a minister casts her lot, on a somewhat consistent basis, either with the old-timers or with the newcomers. On occasion, ministers, through their sermons, will seek to bring the two camps together.

These are people who have been fussing and feuding with each other for years. Their pattern is to find something to fight about. They fight. Then there is a period of truce and resting up. Then they find something else to fight about. There was the argument over who moved the kitchen utensils from where they have always been. There was the debate over the way to do name tags for a covered-dish supper. There was the issue of who moved the coatrack. In a two-cell congregation, the debates over trivial things are virtually unending. The two groups will not come together, simply for the sake of coming together.

Sermons that focus on trying to get the two cells together miss the point. The two cells are already preoccupied with each other. Sermons that are preoccupied with the two cells simply reinforce their preoccupation with each other. Regrettably, such sermons simply further the cleavage between the two cells.

Sermons that stir their longings to serve God's mission help them live beyond themselves. They become less preoccupied with one another and focus more fully on the persons whom they sense God is leading them to serve in mission. Achieving this focus on others is not an easy task. It takes considerable creativity and persistence. Nevertheless, helping people discover the longings to serve that God has planted within them is a more constructive way forward than being preoccupied with the two groups.

The helpful way beyond a two-cell church is to grow a third group. In this way, the focus, the preoccupation is with our mission, not with ourselves. As we discover our longings for God's mission, we become less concerned with status and more interested in service. We live beyond ourselves, and, in doing so, we discover our true selves.

Now, a three-cell congregation still fights, but at least the cells take turns. From time to time, two of the three cells may find themselves in disagreement. The third cell continues with the mission, keeps the balance of power focused on the mission, and helps the other two cells rediscover their invitation and strengths for the mission. At another time, yet another conflict between two of the cells may emerge. The third cell, which may have been involved in an earlier fight, now continues the mission and keeps the balance of power moving toward the mission. So long as they serve, finally, in mission, the three cells will do well with one another.

Whole, Healthy Lives

In a sermon that helps us grow whole, healthy lives in the grace of God, people—with the help of that sermon—discover power to advance their lives. They learn how to lead their lives as well as live them. Regrettably, on rare occasions, a sermon shares anger and an abusive spirit from the pastor. Such sermons are done under the guise of being addressed to commitment and challenge. What they really are is a minister's anger being displaced onto the congregation. Sometimes a sermon encourages a codependent-dependent behavior pattern between the congregation and the minister. The sermon contributes to destructive patterns of behavior. Constructive sermons help us advance, grow, build, and develop the gifts with which God blesses us.

Encouragement

In a sermon that is encouraging, people find confirmation and assurance of their gifts, strengths, and competencies. Under threat, people wither. With encouragement, people grow. Scolding, lamenting, complaining, and whining do not help people advance their lives. Sermons filled with shoulds, oughts, musts, conditions, and stipulations freeze people into doing nothing. When people fear making a mistake, they find that the best way not to make a mistake is to do nothing. Sermons that are invitational and that help people discover the possibilities with which God is blessing them encourage people to grow forward.

Spirit of Compassion

In a sermon that helps people discover a spirit of compassion, people find the love of God. They are overwhelmed with the compassion with which God blesses them. Sometimes there is a conflict in a congregation or a community. The only people I know who do not have conflict are buried in the nearest cemetery, and, sometimes when I walk by late at night, I am not so sure about them. I hear the mutterings and the murmurings. What distinguishes the best of families is not the absence of conflict but the presence of reconciliation, compassion, and willingness to move on.

Regrettably, on occasion a pastor's sermon may seek to pour on a kind of sentimental ooze to somehow soothe the conflict that is raging; the sermon tries to cover it over. This does not help. On occasion, I have heard pastors deliver what I call a mug-wump-swamp sermon. Whatever the issue at hand, the sermon essentially becomes a mug-wump sermon: the minister sits with his mug on one side of the fence and his wump on the other side. In effect, the sermon tries to play both ends against the middle. The minister ends up in a swamp. It is not a helpful sermon. Neither sentimental ooze nor mug-wump sermons illustrate compassion. They evidence conflict repression and conflict avoidance.

People say to me, again and again, "Dr. Callahan, please help us find a pastor who will come and love us and whom we can come to love." The prophets of Israel loved Israel deeply. They wept over Israel. The first step in being helpfully prophetic is to learn to weep, to love deeply and fully the people with whom you serve. Then you can share—with honesty and integrity—a sermon of compassion. Your compassion will stir your people's compassion.

Sense of Community

In a sermon that helps people find a sense of community, people discover roots, place, belonging, and family in God's family. In our time, people look for three things in a congregation: help, hope, and home. People join a congregation, not a denomination. They become part of a family, not members of an institution. They join a movement, not an organization. They search for community, not a committee.

The strength in many sermons is that they create and build community. The sermons encourage a sense of community that has about it a spirit of the grass roots. People discover they belong to a family where there is no higher or lower "status." Yes, there is a diversity of gifts, but none are higher or lower. They all have equal standing in the eyes of God. In a sermon that stirs our sense of community, people know, virtually as the sermon is being preached, that they are one in the Lord, that they have found home.

The Warm Moments of the Sermon

Help your sermon have several warm moments. Space these warm moments out across the length of the sermon. Warm moments are stories of people and events that touch the heart. Warm moments are personal moments in which you share something that has happened or is happening in your own life or the life of another person. You create warm moments as you share your wisdom, your good-fun times, your wrestling with difficult times, or your embarrassing experiences. As you share your new discoveries and excellent mistakes that have helped you grow and develop, you help your people grow.

Warm moments include events of humor and events of sadness. It is in these moments that your congregation discovers who you are and how you are growing and developing in the grace of God.

As we discussed in Chapter Three, we can describe the material in a sermon using a spectrum. We saw that at one end were *simple, stirring, inspiring,* and *emotional,* and on the other, *complex, thoughtful, profound,* and *intellectual.* Warm moments tend to be toward the left end of this spectrum; they tend to be simple, stirring, inspiring. They touch the heart. Your soul responds. Contrast the warm moments with the other end of the spectrum, where the cognitive aspect dominates, the intellect is touched, and your brain responds.

You can use this spectrum to think about a whole season of sermons. My encouragement to you is that on eight out of twelve Sundays, give or take a few, you share sermons that are simple, stirring, and inspiring, that touch the heart. Warm moments are richly present. That leaves four out of the twelve Sundays when you might share a sermon that is more complex, thoughtful, profound, intellectual. God will bless your preaching.

People grow forward as they identify with the warm moments in your sermons. Look at the individuals and families in your congregation—these are the people with whom you are preaching. Do not think of them as the people whom you are preaching "at." You are not preaching "to" them or "down to" them. You are not giving a lecture. You are not reading a term paper to a transient group of people who are students for one semester. You are sharing a sermon, a sign of the grace of God, with a congregation with whom you live and work and share this life.

In our time, when you look at the persons with whom you are living and preaching, you will discover there is a high density of excellent sprinters. There will also be solid marathon runners.

Ours is now a culture of excellent sprinters. I think that invites from us excellent sprinter preaching: the pace of the sermon is faster; the point of the sermon is achieved earlier and needs to be less elusive, less like a vague mystery tale with a wandering plot. The warm moments appear more frequently and with a faster pace.

When you preach with excellent sprinters, preach in an excellent sprinter way. Get to the point in the time at hand. In an earlier, solid marathon runner culture, a minister could plant the small seed of the sermon somewhere in the first five minutes, let it grow slowly, and harvest it thirty minutes later.

We now live in a culture of sound bites and quick closure. We now grow impatient when it takes a full two minutes to download something from the Internet. So let your sermon become more like a series of fast breaks—of strengths and warm moments—down a basketball court, rather than a steady, methodical cross-country run of thirty miles.

Do not put yourself under pressure to deliver a Pulitzer Prize–winning sermon each week. People do not come to worship looking for masterpiece sermons. They do come looking for some help for the week to come.

Ways Forward

I encourage you to advance your preaching by growing your competencies in these four components of structure and flow. The following sequence is a possibility. First, focus on advancing the first three minutes of your sermons. Grow your ability to begin your sermons strongly. Second, give your attention to the last three minutes. Develop the art of closing well. Third, grow your competency to include rich, full strengths in your sermons. Fourth, focus on the warm moments of your sermons. Include more fully your own experience and wisdom as you share your sermons.

The art is to develop your competency with structure and flow in ways that work for you. In the coming three to five months, you can focus on the first three minutes. Then, in the next three to five months, give your attention to advancing the last three minutes, and so on.

Another possibility is to develop the art of structure on a more "sermon-by-sermon" basis. In some sermons, help the first three minutes. Begin well more often. In some sermons, find possibilities for letting the last three minutes end on a high note. In other sermons, focus on advancing the strengths that are fully, richly present. With some sermons, help people discover warm moments more often—times when they draw close with one another in the presence of the grace of God.

Be certain, as best you can, that a given sermon includes at least one of these four components of structure and flow. Not every sermon needs to have *all* the elements of structure and flow in place. Look at the sermon for any given Sunday. Ask yourself, Which one or two of these is naturally present in this coming sermon?

You can advance your understanding of the structure and flow of a sermon with several resources. One way you can do so is to select some person to serve as an editorial coach. Select a mentor, a key leader, a grassroots person, or a gifted preaching pastor. Select someone who has gifts and competencies with structure and flow. Invite him or her to look at five sermons you have recently done in the light of these questions:

How do the first three minutes of this sermon work?

How do the last three minutes of this sermon work?

What are the key strengths in this sermon?

What are the warm moments in this sermon?

Teach your coach which one or two of these you are most interested in having her focus on. At the same time, encourage her to share key suggestions on all four.

You can do this process with one person this year and with another person next year. Or you can invite one person to look at the sermons you have shared during a recent Advent and ask another person for her suggestions on the sermons you have shared during a recent Lent. You can involve a third person at some future time. You can include wisdom and suggestions from four persons, each focusing on one of the four components of structure and flow. Develop editorial coaches who help you grow.

A second way is for you to do your own review of recent sermons, asking yourself these same questions. Periodically take time to study these questions in relation to your recent sermons. I suggest you select five sermons for your study— any five that interest you. Pick five you would have fun with—that have you puzzling as to how the components of structure and flow lived themselves out.

Do not try to study all your sermons. You will get bogged down. You may even develop analysis-paralysis. You run the risk of being caught in a compulsion toward perfectionism. Simply select a few sermons. Study them. You will develop your ability to advance the structure and flow of your preaching. Each new sermon will be improved by the insights you gain.

A third way forward is to gather a one-time team. Yes, this group will meet one time. This is not a weekly or monthly group. You already have enough groups like that in your life to last you four lifetimes.

Invite two, three, or four persons to meet with you. Five is usually too many. You likely do not need that much resourcing, and, with five or more persons, this one-time session would take too long. You could get involved in too many discussions among the group members, and there is the danger that you would get so many suggestions that you would end up acting on none of them.

You are not trying to solve everything about structure and flow in this one-time gathering. You are simply looking for a few excellent ideas and good suggestions you can act on now.

Select persons who are gifted in coaching. Invite them to be in a one-time creativity group with you. Give each person on the team one sermon. Invite them to study the sermon in advance. Encourage them to discover their good ideas on how to advance and improve each of the components: the first three minutes, the last three minutes, the strengths of the sermon, and the warm moments.

With, for example, four persons on your one-time team, you will benefit from their suggestions on four sermons and learn much that will help you grow your competency with the structure and flow of preaching. In some instances, you might give all four sermons to your four-person team. Ask each of them to focus on one. The reason they have the other three is so that they can become familiar with them in advance and, therefore, be in a better position to understand the suggestions shared by the other team members.

A fourth way forward is to focus on the ten strongest Sundays of the year. I encourage you to think of Christmas and Easter Sundays and the eight other Sundays that are your best-attended services of the year. You can decide, for example, that in a given year you want to improve the warm moments of a sermon. Take these ten best Sundays during the year and, if nothing else goes well on those Sundays, let the warm moments of your sermons be helpful in people's lives.

You are creating ten one-time sermons that function as short-term, highly intensive, excellent sprints to assist you in growing forward your competency with one of the components of structure and flow. Further, you are doing so on some of the Sundays that count most in people's lives and destinies.

You will think of other possibilities to advance the structure and flow of your sermons. Pick one of the four components as your focus, and look for specific objectives with which you can advance and improve it. There is benefit for your preaching. Even more important, there is benefit for the people with whom you share your preaching. As you advance the structure and flow of your sermons, more people will richly and fully discover the grace of God in their lives.

9

Outcome

I share with people a basic principle: set the date for the wedding and then work backward.

People who set the date for their wedding have a high tendency to get married. People who never set the date for their wedding hardly ever get married. Once we know the date of the wedding and the nature of the wedding, we know when to have the rehearsal, the rehearsal dinner, and the showers. We know the timing for the gowns, the announcements, the arrangements, and so on. What drives the schedule is the date and nature of the wedding—the outcome we seek to achieve.

The art of long-range planning is not to work from today forward. The art is to see the objective toward which we are heading, set the date for achieving this objective, and then work backward from this date. To be sure, we look forward with anticipation. We think from today forward. There emerges a lively dynamic between where we are heading and where we are now. But mostly we look to the date for the wedding and work backward. Healthy, effective congregations have this spirit in their planning. We see the outcome toward which we are headed, and we work backward to achieve this outcome.

In the same spirit, look forward to the outcome for your sermon and work backward from that. Ministers who see the outcome for their sermon usually *reach* an outcome for the sermon. Ministers who don't see an outcome for their sermon almost never reach an outcome for that sermon. Their sermons wander from here to there and sort of end with a whimper, or they "end" two and three times as, in the midst of preaching the sermon, they now search for some outcome for the sermon.

Ask yourself these questions:

What is the outcome the text is leading me to?

What is the outcome I hope will result from this sermon?

What needs to happen in order to reach this outcome?

Now, I do not mean that we superimpose some artificial construct on the text of the sermon. We do not force some meaning on the text that is foreign to the text. We always begin with the Scripture, the sense of the grace of God, and the awareness that we are surrounded by prayer. We allow the Spirit to guide us in the direction the text leads us.

But it is naive to assume that we come to the text as a blank slate, waiting passively for the text to write its message on our hearts and in our minds. We bring to the text all of who we are, with our strengths and frailties, our despair and our hopes, our compassion and community. We bring our anxieties and fears, our prejudices and pride, our weak sins and our terrible sins. We bring the past we have lived and our expectancies for the future we hope to live.

Sometimes we are conscious of all we bring to the text. Sometimes we are less aware of what we bring. As a consequence, these almost unconscious influences we unwittingly bring to the text force on the text a direction that is unnatural to the text. I am inviting you to be more intentional and conscious of all that you bring to the text. Your sermons will be more helpful.

Further, I invite you, early on, to begin to have in mind—tentatively at least—a result, an outcome to which you sense the text leading you that you hope to achieve with this sermon. Yes, keep open to the text. At the same time, have some direction toward which you are heading. It is somewhat like sailing. We set a destination toward which we are heading, open to the winds and the waves. We tack, change course, and discover a new direction. Let the text lead you. Let the sense of outcome lead you as well. These two are good friends; they go together.

As you pray and puzzle, think and feel a specific sermon, be open to the outcome toward which you are heading. Across the years, people have taught me that these outcomes have been helpful and decisive in their lives:

• Grace
• Wisdom
• Hope
• Mission

For each sermon, consider which of these outcomes will be most helpful, on this Sunday, with the people in your congregation and in your community.

Grace

One possible outcome of preaching is grace. In a given sermon, what people will sense, discover, and come to realize is the grace of God. The sermon becomes a generous gift of grace.

A sermon of grace tends to share the spirit of this text in Matthew 25:35–37: "For I was hungry and you gave me food, I was thirsty and you gave me drink, I was a stranger and you welcomed me, I was naked and you clothed me, I was sick and you visited me, I was in prison and you came to me."

God is this way with us. God cares for our every need. It is amazing how God shares grace with us.

Your sermon helps people discover the remarkable generosity with which God blesses their lives. They come to realize the holy mercy God shares with them. They receive, with astonishment, humility, and gratitude, the loving kindness and abiding compassion that God gives to them. They know the grace of God.

Ask yourself, How can this sermon help people discover the grace of God? What can I say that will lead people to sense, even as I preach, the amazing grace of God? What key points can I share? What illustrations and examples will help? What insights from my own experience will be encouraging?

It is amazing to me. It is a wonder. Who, among humankind, would ever imagine that God would choose that His primary relationship with us would be one of grace? God, being God, can relate to humankind in whatever way He might choose. God could have chosen to be a tyrant and dictator, mean and cruel, aloof and distant. God could have chosen to be capricious and whimsical. God could have chosen to be fickle and inconstant. God chooses a relationship of grace. Amazing!

We are given the precious gift of grace. Our lives are made whole. We draw close to the presence of God. We are in awe and wonder, joy and gratitude. God pours out His grace in our lives. God's grace is like drenching, life-giving rains in a dry, scorching wasteland. With the cooling rains, the desert comes alive. With the blessing of God's grace, we come alive. We live richer, fuller lives, and this is not, finally, our own doing: it is the gift of God.

God shares grace directly with us. God comes to us in Christ, with compassion and new life. God surrounds us with the healing hope of the Holy Spirit. God sends mentors and friends who share grace with us. God helps us discover grace in amazing ways.

In recent years, Julie and I have been blessed with the extraordinary friendship of Michelle and Gabrielle, Great Pyrenees dogs, who are part of our family. Their nature with us is gentle and loving. Their grace and compassion, good spirit and love of fun, have blessed our lives. We are grateful for the years we have shared together. Their unconditional love with us is an amazing example of God's love and grace. We are thankful for all they have taught us and for the wonderful ways they have touched our lives.

Grace comes to us in many ways. Grace transcends all the neat, tidy qualifications we, as humankind, develop. Grace is the ultimate value judgment that tears down all the barriers we construct. Grace moves beyond the rules and regulations, policies and procedures, conditions and stipulations with which we weigh life down. Grace is God's response to all the shoulds and oughts we construct as our conditions for earning our salvation. These constructs squeeze out grace. Grace is the foundation upon which we develop whole, healthy lives.

Sense God's grace in your own life. The more you experience the grace of God, the more naturally you will share sermons whose outcome is grace. It is hard to share a result that one seldom experiences. That is like trying to talk a foreign language without knowing the meaning of the words. That is like trying to lead people to a destination where you have seldom been. Open yourself fully to experience the grace of God.

Live grace. The more you live a life of grace, not law, the more readily your sermons will help people discover grace. Try not to live a life of legalisms. Yes, there are "boundaries" important for us to set so that we do not allow ourselves to be trampled over and so that we do not trample over others. There are acts of consideration and kindness. There are things it is appropriate to do, and there are things not appropriate to do. And these are boundaries of grace, not law.

Living is breathing. Without breathing it is hard to live. Living is grace. Without grace it is hard to live. Grace is as important as breathing. When we live grace, we are alive. When we try to live without grace, we are empty shells of who, with God's grace, we can fully be.

Grow your preaching with grace. Helpful sermons grow out of preparation that is surrounded by the grace of God. It is not so much that people long for the finely crafted phrase or the carefully constructed sentence or the highly sophisticated, heavily intellectual statement, such as "The eschatological significance of this soteriological text has these ecclesiological implications for our time." What people long for is the experience of grace. Let your sermon be an experience of grace. Let the outcome lead people to the grace of God.

Wisdom

One of the primary outcomes of a given sermon can be wisdom—people discover a new way of thinking. Through the experience and wisdom that you share in the sermon, the congregation discovers a new perspective. The result of the sermon is new-found wisdom.

The sermon leads us to discover the possibilities for our lives. The sermon advances our hopes and expectancies. We have a tendency to live either forward or downward toward our expectancies. We discover a new attitude. We examine old assumptions we have held about life and people. New assumptions are advanced and developed. We see life with new wisdom.

In effect, the sermon says, "This is my experience with life. These are other persons' experiences with life. We are simply sharing our wisdom and experience. Learn from us."

Sometimes we share our own learnings and discoveries. Sometimes we share our own excellent mistakes. We have learned from our mistakes, and others can benefit as well.

When we share our own wisdom and experience and, for that matter, when we share the wisdom and experience of others, we do so with gentleness and humility. We do not share our discoveries and insights in a spirit of pride and boasting. There is no bravado, flaunting, or bragging. There is no spirit of haughtiness and superiority. We are humbly grateful to share what we have learned and are continuing to learn in this life's pilgrimage.

We will, in the course of the sermon, share the wisdom and experience of others, as well as our own. However, a sermon is not a long collection of quotations from others. We do not simply go to our files and string together a series of sayings that we have been saving across the years. You can almost tell when a pastor has done that. The only connection between the quotations is that they happen one after another on the same day in the same place.

When we share the wisdom and experience of others, there is a natural fit of our experience and their experience. The common ground of our mutual experiences gives us some wisdom in the living of life. Amidst the ironies and tragedies of life, the sadness and sorrow, the joy and wonder, our experience teaches us there is new life. With wisdom, we can lead whole, healthy lives.

Wisdom is not law and legalisms—shoulds, oughts, or musts. Wisdom is not long lists of bemoanings, lamentings, whinings, and scoldings. Sermons with wisdom are not long, drawn-out lectures by reprimanding scolders. Wisdom does not grow low self-esteem, passive-aggressive behavior, and subliminal forms of resentment. Wisdom is encouraging.

Sermons that focus on wisdom free people from the dock. The result of such sermons is this: people do set sail. They are no longer preoccupied with making a mistake. Ships are meant for sailing, not staying at the dock. We have this one life to live. God invites us to set sail, to live well and fully. Sermons that are invitational, that invite people to their own best wisdom, help people launch whole, healthy lives.

Ask yourself, How can this sermon help people discern the strengths with which God has blessed them? What experiences can I share that will lead people, even as I preach, to new wisdom, to new insights and perceptions about their lives? What key possibilities for their growth can I share? How can this sermon help them claim their strengths? How can this sermon encourage them to expand one of their current strengths and add one new strength?

The sermon that leads to wisdom has about it the spirit of invitation, not demand; of shared experience, not challenge; of lessons well learned in life. The outcome of such a sermon is that people develop a new way of thinking, a new sense of developing their own wisdom.

Hope

One of the outcomes of preaching is what I call handles of help and hope. People live on hope more than memory. Hope is stronger than memory. Memory is strong. Hope is stronger. Take away a person's memories and they become anxious. Take away a person's hopes and they become terrified. Luther said it well: "Everything done in humankind is done on the basis of hope."

Memory is strong. We remember tragic events that mar and scar our lives. We remember sinful events for which we ask God's and others' forgiveness. We remember incidental events; we don't quite know why we remember them, yet we do. We remember celebratory events, good fun, and good times. We remember hope-fulfilling events—those events that decisively fulfilled our deepest yearnings, longings, and hopes. Memory is strong, finally, because memory is about hopes that have happened.

Change is strong. We experience much change in our time. Emerging trends, earthquake shifts, new developments—swift, rapid, and sometimes fleeting—happen virtually every day. Kingdoms rise and fall. Civilizations come and go. Some people are born and some die. People come and leave. People grow and develop. Change abounds.

Conflict is strong. We are sometimes astonished at the conflicts that affect our lives. We experience conflicts across the planet, in our own country, and in our own community. They find their way to us. We find conflict in our work and on our own street. The conflicts in our own family are surprising to us. We hardly ever thought they would happen to us. Sometimes we are amazed at the bizarre forms of conflict in which we have found ourselves.

Four dynamics have impact on our lives: memory, change, conflict, and hope. Memory, change, and conflict abound. Hope is stronger. We live, finally, on hope. All four dynamics have their power in our lives, and the most powerful of the four is hope. Amidst the tragedies and difficulties; the dark nights of depression and despair; the sinfulness, sometimes small, and sometimes, terrible—we live on hope. There is something in the human spirit, as a gift from God, that invites us to look to the coming of hope in our lives.

Indeed, people come to a service of worship longing for, looking for, hope for the week to come. To be sure, they want some help with the week that has been and with the past of their own lives. They do look for forgiveness and reconciliation for what has been. And they look for "moving on." They want some sense that there is hope for their future. They want confirmation and assurance that some of their best days, weeks, and years are before them, not behind them.

A few sermons live in the past. That is, those sermons are built, regrettably, on the false notion that people live in the past, and the purpose of the sermon is to drag them, albeit reluctant and screaming, into the present. Most people do not live in the past. A few do, perhaps. Most people live in the present and the future. Their hopes and expectancies shape how they behave in the present.

At Piney Grove church, Mrs. Lott and I were visiting after the service on Sunday. It was a wonderful fall day, with the leaves turning and the color on the trees. We had had a good worship service. The pastor had shared a solid sermon. Most people had gone. It hadn't taken that long. There weren't that many people to go.

In the midst of our good-fun conversation, she said to me, "You know, Dr. Callahan, I do everything I do based on whether or not it will help me be part of God's Kingdom in the next life." Mrs. Lott was not living in the past. She was living, in hope, toward the future. She saw her sources of hope in the next life, beyond the river.

We look for hope where we can find it. We seek sources of hope in the present, the immediate future, the distant future, and the next-life future. If we cannot find hope in the present, we look to the immediate future. If we cannot see it there, we look to the distant future or the next-life future. We postpone our hopes down the road.

Mrs. Lott was saying that the sources of hope that had worked for her in the present and immediate future were no longer working so well. Her husband, retired from the farm, rattled around the house each day, not knowing quite what to do. Her mother was dying of cancer in a nearby nursing home. Strange, new people now lived up and down Flowery Springs Road. The ways she had found sources of hope in the present were no longer working for her. She was living in hope for the next life.

Many congregations sing such songs as "We Shall Gather at the River," "Dwelling in Beulah Land," "In the Sweet Bye and Bye." These are not hymns of the past. These are hymns of hope, looking to the life to come. Their power is in their hope.

Ask yourself, How can this sermon help people discover hope for their lives now? What can I say that will lead people to experience, even as I preach, a sense of confidence and assurance about their future? What key insights can I suggest? What handles of help and hope can I share? What stories and analogies will help? What sharings from my own experience will be hope-fulfilling with my congregation?

The outcome, the result, of your sermon will be that people discover specific, concrete handles they can grasp. They can use them now, this very day. These handles of hope help people grow forward their lives. They give assurance and encourage a healthy confidence in people's present and their future.

Your sermon heals emotions, stirs motivations, advances hope. As a result of your sermon, people discover possibilities for living with hope. They find they can grow and develop, advance and build their own lives. They move forward with a strong sense of hope.

Mission

One possible outcome of preaching is a sense of mission. People discover the purpose for their lives. They discover the mission to which God invites them. Their behavior moves forward. They put new habits in place.

We are here for a reason. We are here for a purpose. We are here for a mission. Our lives are the gift of God. As we discover a sense of purpose and mission, we grow forward as whole, healthy persons.

Generally speaking, three possibilities of preaching exist:

- Deductive: the sermon brings the Word to the congregation.
- Inductive: the sermon brings the congregation to the Word.
- Mission: the sermon brings the person, the congregation, to the mission.

All three possibilities have value. All three are helpful.

On a given Sunday your sermon, *deductively*, brings the Word to the congregation.

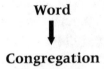

Your sermon begins with the text. In a deductive fashion, step by step, you help the people in your congregation discover the implications of the text for their lives.

On yet another Sunday, your sermon, *inductively*, may lead people to the Word.

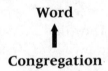

Your sermon begins with the congregation. In an intuitive and inductive manner, you lead your people to discover the text.

On yet another Sunday, your sermon, with a focus on *mission*, brings the people of your congregation to the world. *Mission* preaching, in our time, is most helpful. The outcome of the sermon is that people discover the mission in the world to which God is inviting them.

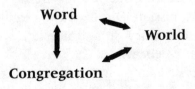

The starting point of God's grace is the world. We live in the world. We come from the world. The starting point of the sermon is the world. In the sermon, we discover the grace of God in the world. We discover the purpose for our life. We live this purpose out in the world, in mission with specific human hurts and hopes. In mission preaching, there is a healthy interaction between world, Word, and congregation.

Even today, some sermons tend to assume a churched culture. On occasion, I find myself listening to such a sermon, and I confess I have preached my own fair share. I am struck with the fact that such sermons tend to be "inside-the-church" sermons. They tend to focus on matters inside the organization. Their frame of reference is primarily the congregation and the Word.

Such sermons focus on helping people live inside the church. The assumption is that the "real world" is the church. These sermons suggest ways to be active in the church, participate in its groupings, and serve on its committees. It is almost as if the world does not exist. Sometimes the sermon acknowledges the world, but it is looking out from the church on the world.

The day of church preaching is over. The day of mission preaching has come. As we discussed in Chapter One, we can no longer assume a congregation's lifelong Christian background and upbringing, let alone a churched culture. We are no longer preaching to get people to "come back" to church. We are now preaching with persons who have never "been" to come "back."

The view of the sermon begins where people begin—in the world. The focal point of the sermon is living in the world. The frame of reference is the world, not the church. The mission is not the church. The mission is in the world. We are not invited to save the church. We are invited to serve the world.

Both deductive and inductive preaching, at their best, share a similar spirit. The tendency, in a churched culture, however, was to drift toward a focus inside the church. Sermons were preoccupied with the institutional well-being of the church as an organization. In a time of social conformity when the culture delivered people to the church, the drift toward institutional preaching was perhaps understandable.

In mission preaching, the focus, the starting point, the primary frame of reference is the world. The purpose of the preaching is to help people live in the world. It is more like in the early days with the disciples, when there were no churches. The only place the preaching could be shared was in the world. There were no churches to stay inside of. That was like the frontier, pioneering mission fields of our day. The frame of reference is the world, and the mission to which God invites us is this world.

All three possibilities for preaching are helpful. In any given sermon, one of these three can live itself out. Sometimes your preaching can focus on deductive preaching; your sermon will bring the Word to the congregation. At other times, your sermon can focus on inductive preaching; your sermon will bring the congregation to the Word. My hope is that your preaching frequently will focus on mission preaching. In this way, you will bring the congregation to the mission.

In our time, helpful preaching brings the people of God and the Word of God to the mission of God. The purpose of preaching is to lead God's people to mission in the community and the world. Preaching leads people to discover the mission and purpose for their lives.

Ask yourself, How can this sermon help people discover the purpose for their lives? What can I say that will lead people to experience, even as I preach, a sense of mission and purpose? What key insights can I suggest? To what human hurts and hopes can I point them? What examples of mission in the world can I lift up? What sharings from my own sense of mission and purpose will be helpful with my congregation?

Hearing mission preaching, people discover their deep longings to serve. They discover a sense of purpose for their lives. They discover, within themselves, a stirring, moving compassion. They have a rich, full passion that their lives will count well. Quietly, they live whole, healthy lives of purpose and mission. They share in the mission of God. They share in the future to which God invites us.

Ways Forward

The purpose of preaching is to help people discover grace, wisdom, hope, and mission in their lives. The purpose of preaching is not to save institutions, recruit teachers, or raise money. The purpose of preaching is to save people, to shepherd people, to help people, to serve people.

Outcome preaching begins at the end and works backward. Begin your sermon at the end. Start with the behavior outcome you hope this sermon will bring about. Then allow the desired outcome to shape your preparation. The end shapes the beginning. Certainly, how you begin will also shape how you end. Decide where you want to be at the end and work backward from there.

Share with the people of your congregation the *outcome* to which the sermon is inviting them. Share—with a spirit of compassion and a sense of community—*why* you hope they will advance in this manner. Share *how* they can achieve this outcome in their lives. Deliver *encouragement* and positive reinforcement. Lead them to their strengths.

I encourage you to deliver outcome preaching rather than problem-based preaching. A helpful sermon is not fifteen minutes of problem diagnosis and three minutes of glowing generalities—"Jesus is the answer." Yes, Jesus is the answer, and Jesus shared more than this with us. Jesus shared concrete ways forward. Most people know their problems pretty well. They do not come looking for problem analysis. They come looking for ways forward, so that their life will count, so that, at the end of their days, they can look back and know that their life made a difference.

Outcome preaching begins with and builds on these steps: *way, why, how,* and *encouragement.* Outcome preaching is invitational. The sermon suggests good news by sharing

Here is *a way forward* for your life.

Here is *why* this will be helpful with you and others.

Here is *how* you can advance this strength in your life.

Here is the *encouragement* that will help you, this day, move forward.

Across the years, I have heard many different sermons. A teaching sermon has an educational, instructional focus. A shepherding sermon has a pastoral concern. A motivational sermon seeks to stir and inspire people. An elocutionary sermon seeks to share the message through the alliteration and poetry of the words.

I have experienced muddled, confused sermons. It is hard to know where these sermons are heading, if anywhere. They remind me of Alice in Wonderland, who asks, "Which road will I take?" The Cheshire Cat responds with the question, "Where are you headed?" Alice says, "I don't know." The Cat says, "Then it won't matter which road you take." Some sermons are like that; they head everywhere and nowhere.

I have also experienced sermons that are strings of quotations, one quotation after another. You can almost see the card file and the index on the pastor's desk. In more recent times, he may sit at his computer, with the card file and index now stored there. He pulls from here and there. He puts together a lengthy list of quotations, with some filler in between, that he preaches as a sermon.

On occasion, I have listened to sermons of fury. The preacher, in anger and admonition, in a furious kind of way, tries to scare and frighten the people toward some new direction. A few sermons are simply a barren desert. A few are so much fluff and flimsy. It is so much cotton candy, froth, and fizz. Such sermons do not give people handles of help and hope.

Some sermons are managerial, preoccupied with policies and procedures. Some are institutional, concerned with saving the organization. Some are apocalyptic, almost manufacturing one crisis after another. All of these are of lesser value. They have had their day.

Mostly, your congregation wants to know *your* wisdom and experience, *your* sense of grace and hope, *your* direction of mission. Your people would like to know these things *from your head and your heart*. They value the sermons you share. They find them helpful in their lives.

In outcome preaching, we know this:

The members of the congregation experience grace.

People discover wisdom.

Their emotions are stirred.

Behavior moves forward.

The sermon is helpful.

We become whole, healthy persons in the grace of God.

Outcome preaching makes a difference. People's lives are advanced. Mission happens.

On a given Sunday, the focus of your sermon may be on grace. On another Sunday, the focus may be on wisdom. On another Sunday, the major emphasis may be on hope. On yet another Sunday, the focus may be on mission. The primary focus is on one of the four. The other three will be present. These four outcomes are in dynamic interaction with one another. Be at peace about trying to focus on all four in a sermon. You do not need to do so. Focus on one outcome, one result. The other three will be there, supporting and encouraging.

Outcome preaching is behavior preaching. It is good news preaching. It is parable preaching. The sermon shares just enough of the grace of God, just enough wisdom and experience, just enough handles of help and hope, just enough in the way of mission and purpose that people can discover, for themselves, the direction in which they plan to head as they live whole, healthy lives in the grace of God.

10
Creating a New Beginning

Preaching is an art. Preaching is an art you can nurture and grow by thoughtful learning and continuing development. A few people may be "born" preachers. For them, preaching seems to come naturally and effortlessly. There is a quiet grace to their preaching. There is confidence and assurance in what they do.

For every "born" preacher I know, I know hundreds who have learned—and are continuing to learn—the art of preaching. They intentionally develop some of the eight areas we have discussed. Good fun and hard work, grace and creativity advance their competencies for preaching. Their focus is on preaching that is helpful in people's lives and destinies in the grace of God.

As you preach, and as you continue to advance your preaching, you will find the following questions helpful. I encourage you to focus on *some* of these questions for each sermon. Do not allow a compulsion toward perfectionism to take hold so that you end up asking yourself all the questions about each sermon. It is more like this: as I look at the sermon I am planning to share this Sunday, I can answer these specific questions in a positive manner. In a good-fun, discovering, growing spirit, prayerfully and with compassion, you can use these questions to help you advance the sermon you are planning to share this week:

- Does the sermon have a sense of presence?
- Does the sermon share the gospel of grace and good news?
- Is the sermon well prepared?
- Does the sermon draw on a rich array of experience and resources?
- Does the sermon share wisdom for everyday, ordinary life? Is it practical?
- Does the sermon advance the social structures of our time?
- Is the sermon well delivered?
- Is the sermon attractive, warm, and inviting?
- Does the sermon lead people to a spirit of compassion and a sense of community?
- Is the sermon genuinely helpful?
- Does the sermon advance people's lives and destinies in whole, healthy ways?
- Does the sermon serve God's mission?
- Does the sermon draw people closer to the grace of God?

Once you select from the eight possibilities the one or two you look forward to developing, you will be in a strong position to know which of these questions to ask yourself more frequently. Certainly, all the questions are helpful. Let a given sermon live out some of the questions in a positive spirit.

Grow Your Preaching

In our preaching, we are inviting people to grow and develop their lives. We can grow and develop our preaching in this same spirit. If people can advance and grow themselves in something as complex as life, we can do so in our preaching. It is awkward to invite people, in our sermons, to leave off old ways and learn new ways when, Sunday after Sunday, our own preaching continues in the same old pattern. As people see us growing our preaching, it gives them the confidence and assurance that they can grow their lives as well.

People long for preaching that leads them to a theology of service, not a theology of survival. In their daily lives, they already have experienced enough of an institutional survival mentality to last them a long time. They are looking for more than that.

They are interested in preaching that helps them grow whole, healthy lives. They are less preoccupied by whether a given church is growing bigger. In their own work, they have experienced an emphasis on that long enough. Preaching that is concerned primarily with "inside the church" does not help people with their lives. People do not have a compelling interest in saving some institution. They are interested in their lives counting for more than that.

People are interested in preaching that helps them with possibilities for their lives. They are less interested in problem-centered preaching. They have some grasp of the problems with which they wrestle; they understand their problems reasonably well. They have the wisdom to come to church looking for possibilities forward. Many people have already done a solid job of analyzing their problems. What helps them are sermons that spend a few minutes setting forth the problem and then devote the majority of the sermon to sharing ways forward.

People long for preaching that advances their lives. They are not especially looking for "exciting" preaching or for "great" preaching. By the same token, they are not drawn to "boring" preaching. People tend to shy away from sermons that are boring, for two reasons. First, the sermons are boring.

Second, people innately sense that pastors who share boring sermons are persons who are still wrestling with low self-esteem, who are not growing in their own lives.

When we have the sense of solid self-esteem, we share helpful sermons. The key is to grow forward, with the grace of God, one's solid self-esteem. That helps everyone in the congregation who is wrestling with low self-esteem. When we are growing in our own lives and are growing and developing our preaching, we deliver stirring, inspiring, helpful sermons. We are discovering our creativity both in our life and in our preaching.

We bring all we are, all we have learned, and all we are learning to our preaching. We bring our openness and inclusiveness, our anxieties and fears. We bring our prejudices and closed-mindedness, our favorite themes and pet peeves. We bring our own sinfulness and weariness, and we bring our best creativity and imagination. We bring our ability to be proactive and intentional, our capacity to be purposeful and discerning about where we are headed.

This is foundational:

How you grow yourself shapes how you grow your preaching. How you grow your preaching shapes how you grow yourself.

When you maintain healthy habits in your personal growth, you will have healthy habits in growing your preaching. We gain a sense of direction about where we are headed in our lives precisely when we decide the behavior outcome we want to grow and develop, advance and build. Then we work backward from that objective. What is true for preaching is also true for living. What is true for living is also true for preaching.

Growing your preaching is like growing your life. Start with the behavior outcome you want to achieve in your preaching. What do you want your preaching to sound like, look like, feel like, and be like in three months? Five months? One year?

Two principles are true in growing your preaching:

1. How you envision the end shapes how you begin.

2. How you begin your growth shapes how you end up.

In your growth plan, decide where you want to end up. Then work backward from there to plan your specific growth objectives. Act on your plan now. You will grow your preaching. You will grow your life.

Purposefully advancing your preaching is among the most important practices in your life. As you grow your preaching, you advance your life. These key steps help in advancing your preaching:

- Claim your strengths
- Expand one current strength
- Add one new strength
- Act on your future

Claim Your Strengths

This is your first step. Look at the eight possibilities and at your own preaching. Evaluate which are your lead strengths. I encourage you to think of ministers whose preaching is solid and helpful, whose preaching you trust and respect. Discern where their preaching stands in relation to each of these eight possibilities and decide, in comparison with them, where your strengths are. Now, claim your strengths.

God encourages us to claim our strengths. When we claim our strengths, we claim God's gifts. When we deny our strengths, we deny God's gifts. If we do not claim our strengths for preaching, we can hardly help people claim their strengths for living whole, healthy lives in the grace of God. When you claim your strengths for preaching, you are in an excellent position to help people claim their strengths for living.

A strength would be rated as an 8, 9, or 10 on a scale of 1 to 10. Look at the "Possibilities for Growing Your Preaching" chart. Think about your preaching and others' preaching. Draw one line under each of the strengths that, for your preaching, is clearly an 8, 9, or 10. Note well: look for the strengths you really have. If you look for the strengths you *wish* you had, you will miss the strengths you *do* have.

This is not the time to do a complete assessment of where you are on each of the eight. Do not focus on the ones you think are your weakest weaknesses. Begin with God. Begin with the gifts God gives you. Begin with your strengths and underline them on the chart.

Expand One Current Strength

The second step is to select one of your current strengths to expand. The principle is to build on your strengths. Take an 8 and grow it to a 9 or 10, expanding one of your current

Possibilities for Growing Your Preaching

PRESENCE	MOTIVATION
1 2 3 4 5 6 7 8 9 10	1 2 3 4 5 6 7 8 9 10
PREPARATION	DELIVERY
1 2 3 4 5 6 7 8 9 10	1 2 3 4 5 6 7 8 9 10
RESOURCES	STRUCTURE
1 2 3 4 5 6 7 8 9 10	1 2 3 4 5 6 7 8 9 10
CONTENT	OUTCOME
1 2 3 4 5 6 7 8 9 10	1 2 3 4 5 6 7 8 9 10

strengths. Grow it forward. Take care to expand a strength you really *have*, not one you *wish* you had. Look at what you are currently doing well—at the lead strengths you rated 8 or better. Select one you plan to expand to a 9 or 10.

Progress is more helpful than perfection. Do better what you do best. You are looking for evidence of progress rather than trying for the "perfect 10." The compulsion toward perfection can lead us astray here, causing us to set a goal too high. If we give in to our perfection-seeking tendencies, we will end up procrastinating once again. Be realistic. Choose a reasonable goal rather than a perfectionistic one.

In such recovery programs as AA and Al-Anon, people work their Twelve Step program one step at a time, one day at a time. If alcoholics can grow forward their lives beyond something as tough as the difficulty of alcoholism by maintaining a focus on progressing through one step at a time, one day at a time, we can progress in our preaching one step at a time as well.

Thus, look at each of the strengths you have underlined in the chart "Possibilities for Growing Your Preaching." Choose one you want to focus your progress on. Draw a second line under the one current strength you plan in the immediate future to expand—to advance and develop.

Add One New Strength

Now, the third step: add a new strength that builds on and complements the current strengths you have in place and the one current strength you have decided to expand. God helps us add new strengths. Pray about your plan. Discuss it with wise, trusted mentors. Your new strength is like a new, close friend whom you would like to have be part of your life.

In adding a new strength in your preaching, do not look to your weakest points—this places you in a poor position to tackle your weaknesses. You might eventually grow a weak area forward, but it would take considerable effort and difficulty. Do not head to your weakest area. Grow forward where you can grow forward.

This is the time in the process to do a thoughtful assessment of all eight possibilities. Look at the chart. You have already underlined your lead strengths. You have already drawn another line under the one current strength to expand. Now is the time to look at all the others. With your best wisdom and experience, assess where you are on each of them. Circle your ratings on the preceding chart.

Let us look at an illustration. The next figure shows an example of a pastor's completed chart. This pastor had earlier, in the first step, discovered his lead strengths: Content is an 8, Motivation is an 8, and Structure is an 8. He decided to expand his strength in Structure. He drew a second line under it. In the third step, he rated his preaching in the remaining areas as follows: Presence is a 3, Preparation is a 7, Resources is a 6, Delivery is a 5, and Outcome is a 2. He decided to add Preparation as a new strength. He circled that possibility on his chart.

Possibilities for Growing Your Preaching

PRESENCE
1 2 (3) 4 5 6 7 8 9 10

MOTIVATION
1 2 3 4 5 6 7 (8) 9 10

(PREPARATION)
1 2 3 4 5 6 (7) 8 9 10

DELIVERY
1 2 3 4 (5) 6 7 8 9 10

RESOURCES
1 2 3 4 5 (6) 7 8 9 10

STRUCTURE
1 2 3 4 5 6 7 (8) 9 10

CONTENT
1 2 3 4 5 6 7 (8) 9 10

OUTCOME
1 (2) 3 4 5 6 7 8 9 10

As you evaluate yourself, you will discover you have some midrange strengths, rating as a 5, 6, or 7. You will find some weaknesses; they rate as a 1, 2, 3, or 4. Your midrange strengths are on their way toward improvement. They are not yet full strengths. With modest effort, you can grow them as new full strengths.

The key in this third step is to concentrate on improving your midrange strengths. Having done so, you can later select a weaker area. You can advance your preaching more easily by avoiding any focus on a weakness, a 1 through 4. When you decide which possibility you want to add, circle it on your "Possibilities for Growing Your Preaching" chart.

Add the one new strength you *can* add. Not the one you think you *should* add. Or worse, the one *someone else* thinks you should add. The art is to go forward where you *can* go forward. Build on your strengths. Do better what you do best. Add one new strength. Now you are in the strongest position to tackle any weakness.

Act on Your Future

The final step is action. Act on your two possibilities—the one you are expanding and the one you are adding—in ways that match what you have *fun* doing. Consider your everyday-life activities, the ones you genuinely have fun doing. Think of the activities in which you are most alive and energized, most relaxed and at peace.

I frequently invite people to a conversation by saying, "Share with me what you have fun doing." People come alive as they describe what they have fun doing; people also teach me that hardly anyone invites them to think in these terms. Across the years, I have shared in some wonderful conversations.

I am convinced of this: *what we have fun doing is God's way of teaching us our strengths.* Picture what you have fun doing in daily life. Now, grow your two possibilities in ways that match what you have fun doing.

Act on your two possibilities in ways that match *all* your competencies. Yes, consider your gifts in preaching. Further, think of your competencies as a person, as a pastor, in your family life, in your interests and hobbies, and in everyday life. Look at the whole of who you are and the whole of who you are growing yourself to be. Advance your two possibilities, matching your present and growing competencies.

As you advance your preaching, it will have increasing value in your whole community. It will touch people's lives both in your congregation and in your community. You will be a source of help in the whole of the mission field God gives you. You will help the human hurts and hopes present in your community, the ones with which you have longings to help.

With a spirit of spontaneity and creativity, grow forward the two possibilities you sense God is inviting you to improve. God is drawing you forward. God yearns and longs for your preaching to be even more helpful in people's lives and destinies.

Other people can share wisdom and encouragement; only you can grow yourself forward. Finally, you are the one who can grow you. Moreover, you are the best person to grow you. Although we sometimes wish other people would do our growing for us, we have no ownership in what other people do for us. We have ownership in what we do to advance ourselves.

You are the best person to decide your growth. Choose the best sequence for the growth and development of your preaching. Select one of the two possibilities to focus on first; I encourage you not to focus on two at the same time. Expand a current strength first before you have the fun of adding a new strength.

While, for your own reasons, you may decide to reverse the order and add a new strength first and expand a current strength second, most often I encourage you to do better what you already do best. Thus I encourage you to expand first, to have the fun of developing momentum in your growth, then to add a new strength after that.

Choose the best time period for your focus on each of your two possibilities. Based on your wisdom and what you would have fun doing, you might invest three to five months in advancing each possibility you have selected. Although your concentration will be on developing one major area, you will also be advancing and improving the other areas—I call this a spillover effect. Helpful growth in one area spills over, naturally and almost effortlessly, into growth in some of the other areas.

The art is to focus on one possibility. Create a simple action plan. Significantly advance your growth. Look at the suggestions in each chapter. Discover the suggestions that match well with who you are and what you have fun doing.

For example, you might decide one possibility you plan to grow is Resources. To develop resources, you plan to put into place resource teams for Advent and Lent, participate in a Bible-study group in the community, and gather a prayer group that will be helpful and supportive in your preaching.

You might determine that Preparation is one strength you plan to expand. As an excellent sprinter, you put in place four days to plan for the coming three months and create a more constructive, less distracting setting in which to do your sermon preparation.

You may decide to add a newfound strength in Delivery. You plan to have a speech coach work with you for an intensive series of coaching sessions. You plan to be part of a Toast-masters group for a five-month period. You plan to develop your capabilities in community speaking.

Be specific in your growth objectives. Develop a series of one-time actions that each advance one possibility. Put in place a realistic, achievable action plan. This is how you will grow your way forward. You will be acting on your future, and you will become the future you have decided for yourself. You will grow your preaching.

Words count. Words make a difference. Words heal, give hope. Words hurt, do damage. Words cause armies to march, empires to come and go, civilizations to rise and fall. Words bring peace. Words give life, like water in a desert. The sacrament of preaching is decisive in people's lives.

By grace, we preach grace, and this, finally, is not our own doing: it is the gift of God. God gives you the gift of grace so that you can grow.

God gives you a new beginning. God gives you a new age of mission. God invites you to advance your preaching. God surrounds you with His inviting, compelling grace and His quiet, encouraging presence. God plants within you yearnings and longings, impulses, aspirations, and hopes.

God is blessing your preaching. God blesses you in your life. God is giving you a new beginning; now you can give yourself a new beginning. I pray your preaching will be increasingly helpful in people's lives and destinies, that your sermons will help them lead whole, healthy lives.

Through your preaching, may your people discover the grace of God, the compassion of Christ, and the healing hope of the Holy Spirit. May they discover a new beginning for their lives. May your preaching touch their lives with the grace of God.

The Author

Kennon L. Callahan is today's most sought-after church consultant and a powerful preacher in his own right. He is best known for *Twelve Keys to an Effective Church,* which pioneered a widely acclaimed church renewal movement. He has authored eleven other books and is a beloved public speaker. He has served both rural and urban congregations and taught at Emory University. His recent book *Twelve Keys for Living* (Jossey-Bass, 1998) is an excellent companion to *Preaching Grace.*

He divides his time among speaking, consulting, and writing. He and his wife, Julie, enjoy the outdoors, quilting, hiking, painting, and camping.

Index

Christmas, 43, 141

Churched culture: decline of, 2, 7–9, 155; great preachers in, 5; inside-the-church shepherding of, 51; institutional membership vows of, 96; sacrament in, 12

Churched-culture preaching, 3; conformity in, 13–14; homiletic methods of, 5, 13, 42, 51. *See also* Preaching

"Clear desk" principle, 47

Closure, 128–130

Coaching: editorial, 139–141; by mentors, 25–26; speech, 104, 117–119, 120, 121

Codependency, 2, 107, 108, 130, 134

Cognitive level, 42, 137

Commitment: as displaced anger, 100–101, 134; as motivation, 90, 95–98, 101; motivational match or gap on, 91–93

Committees, 89

Community: as motivation, 89, 93–100; motivational match or gap on, 91–93; preaching for sense of, 93–100, 136; research team members in, 58–59; search for, 79; shepherding in, 50–51

Community groups: influential, 64–65; learnings available from, 64; least powerful, 65; participation in, 62–65; practicing delivery skills with, 115–117; as resources, 62–65; types of, 63

Community spaces, sermon preparation in, 44–45, 46

Compassion: challenging people to, 98; facial expression and, 108; as motivation, 89, 93–98; motivational match or gap on, 91–93, 98–100; preaching on/for, 93–101, 108, 127–128, 135

Competencies, healthy, 68–69

Complexity: in content, 76–78; in preparation, 42–43

Confidence, 17, 21–22, 23. *See also* Presence

Conflict: within congregations, 132–134; hope and, 151; and preaching compassion, 135

Conformity, 13–14

Congregations: bridging with, 28–30; cultural shifts and, 80–81; energies of, at beginning versus end of sermon, 126; excellent sprinters and solid marathon runners in, 38; high-compassion and high-commitment, 97; motivational match or gap with, 91–93, 98; old-timers versus newcomers in, 132–134; one-cell, 132; three-cell, 133–134; two-cell, 132–133

Constantine, Emperor, 11–12

Content, 71–86; development of, 71–84; of foundational life searches, 78–80; importance of, 71; keys to living as, 77–78, 85–86; long-term plan for advancing, 84–86; major cultural shifts and, 80–84; Scripture in, 72–75, 85; singular focus of, 75–78

I Corinthians 13, 97

Council of Nicaea, 12

Criticism, 15–16

Cultural shifts: Christian movement and, 2–4; to excellent sprinter culture, 37, 81–82, 86; hope and, 151; to informational, technological culture, 37, 81; to intergalactic worldview, 83–84; listed, 80; mission field and, 2–4; to movement orientation, 82–83; sermon content and, 80–84, 86. *See also* Excellent sprinters; Mission field

D

Dave (motivational story), 87–88

David (research team story), 57

Deductive sermon, 154, 156

Delivery, 103–122; of beginning of sermon, 105, 106–108, 124–128; coaching for, 104, 117–119, 120, 121; confident, 103, 114; dynamics of, 105–115; of end of sermon,